To my close and long time
friend,

I hope you enjoy reading
the book you helped review +
that we continue to
enrich each other both
professionally + personally
for many more years.

Love,

WOMEN AND DISABILITY

WOMEN AND DISABILITY
The Double Handicap

Edited by

Mary Jo Deegan and Nancy A. Brooks

Foreword by
Rose Lynn Sherr and Beatrice A. Wright

Transaction Books
New Brunswick (U.S.A.) and Oxford (U.K.)

Library of Congress Catalog Number: 84-2618
ISBN: 0-88738-017-4 (cloth)
Printed in the United States of America

Library of Congress Cataloging in Publication Data
Main entry under title:

Women and disability.
   1. Physically handicapped women—Addresses, essays,
lectures.   2. Discrimination against women—Addresses, essays,
lectures.   I. Deegan, Mary Jo, 1946-   . II. Brooks, Nancy A., 1943-
HV3021.W66W66   1985   362.4'088042   84-2618
ISBN 0-88738-017-4

    A significant number of chapters in this book first appeared in *The Journal
of Sociology and Social Welfare*, Vol. VIII, No. 2, July 1983, pp. 233–375.
This includes the chapters by Fine and Asch, Becker and Jauregui, Kolb,
Deegan, Kutza, Kutner and Gray, Saxton, McCharen and Earp, and Shaul,
Dowling, and Laden. We thank the journal staff for their support and interest
in this project.
    Most of the chapters previously published have been revised, reedited, and
somewhat altered for the present volume.

To

MARJORIE STAMM
and
JOHN BROOKS

Contents

List of Tables

Figure

Foreword

Rose Lynn Sherr and Beatrice A. Wright

This volume opens up a new area in the literature concerning disability. The seriousness of the lack of recognition of the special needs of women who have disabilities comes through time and again as one reads the various chapters. Some of the chapters provide new levels of understanding and analysis, and some point the way to profitable areas of research. As a collection, this volume makes obvious the need for intervention in the political, social, psychological, and medical domains. In their correspondence with us the editors had noted that, conforming to the requirements of scientific writing, the material was presented nonemotionally. Yet as we read the book, we were shaken and astounded by it.

Our astonishment was due partially to a growing awareness of our own oblivion to the issues presented. Despite our long professional involvement in the field of rehabilitation psychology and our appreciation of a feminist viewpoint, we had been remarkably unaware of the unique issues of women with disabilities. Clearly, we are not alone. The authors provide impressive evidence of the dearth of recognition of these issues by investigators, program planners, clinicans, and most of the world.

Thus, beyond the obvious contribution of the book to the professional literature, an even greater value may lie in its potential for raising the consciousness of its readers to the special status of women with disabilities as a minority group experiencing multiple sources and forms of discrimination. The importance of this consciousness-raising applies to persons involved in making public policy and to the academic and professional rehabilitation communities. It applies to women and men with disabilities. It applies to society as a whole.

The heightened consciousness is essential because the special needs of women with disabilities have been disregarded in a wide variety of vital areas. Consider issues pertaining to women as wives and mothers. What is needed are women with disabilities to serve as role models, but the social support systems traditionally available to women concern problems of able-bodied women in general, not the special problems of women who have disabilities. Although the women's movement has provided additional role supports for women, it also has not been concerned with the special needs of women with disabilities. It is encouraging to learn from the chapters presented in this volume that there have been beginnings of networks and support systems for women with disabilities to deal with various aspects of living.

In the area of health, the volume convincingly documents the notable lack in the medical literature of studies of pregnancy among women who have specific disabilities. Also lacking are studies of the effects on female sexuality of such conditions as renal disease and diabetes, although the sexual functioning of men with these diseases has been researched. Similarly, the effects on male sexual functioning of medication to control hypertension are recognized, but not the effects on women's sexual functioning.

On the economic front, the social structures established on behalf of people who have a disability have not taken into account the fact that women have traditionally been disadvantaged in the marketplace by sex stereotypes and depressed earnings. The programs, therefore, have not seriously considered the particular circumstances of women with disabilities. Consequently, the Federal-State Vocational Rehabilitation System and the regulations concerning disability benefits under Social Security provide less adequately for women than for men.

The past 20 years have brought increased awareness of the special issues concerning various disadvantaged groups, including racial and ethnic minorities, people with disabilities, women, and older persons. The result has been the occurrence of notable changes in policy and practice on the part of government and the private sector to redress legitimate grievances, and changes in research and technical orientation. The present volume promises to catalyze a similar advance with regard to women with disabilities.

Preface

Physically disabled women are a population close to the minds and hearts of the editors and authors of this text. In one form or another, we have felt the effects of discrimination and stigmatization on the lives of disabled women whom we have loved and admired. This book, then, is not a dispassionate analysis of yet another social problem but a reflection of a lived reality that we know well. It is with great joy and a sense of achievement that we are able to participate in the writing and editing of this collective task.

As editors we have the privilege of singling out not only the chapter contributors but others whose work is less visible but nonetheless vital. We owe special thanks to Norman Goroff, a former editor of *The Journal of Sociology and Social Welfare*. He introduced the editors to each other and encouraged us to work together for a special issue of the journal. After a rather slow start, we found that we did, indeed, share a number of mutual interests. During a series of telephone conversations, we decided on this topic of physically disabled women. Bob Leighninger, who succeeded Norman Goroff as the editor of the journal, continued the good spirit and support of his predecessor. Both of us have received support from our respective Deans who supplied us with funds for advertisements, mailing, xeroxing, and telephone calls. Therefore, we give a special note of thanks to Max Larsen, the former Dean of Arts and Sciences at the University of Nebraska-Lincoln and to Lloyd Benningfield, the Dean of the Graduate School at Wichita State University. The Nebraska Research Council generously provided the funds needed for the final preparation of the mansucript. This support came at a crucial point in the manuscript process enabling us to spend more time on the content of the work rather than its physical production. Michael R. Hill, Laurie Workman Eells, and Sharon Selvage entered the manuscript on the computer, and they are heartily thanked for their great service, support, and constructive criticisms. We would also like to thank Margaret Zahn for supplying us with the names of sociologists who were members of the subsection on disability in the American Sociological Association's medical section. The following individuals also served as reviewers of the manuscripts; their aid and knowledge were invaluable: Gary Albrecht, Elwin Barrett, Jane Bogel, Thomasina Borkman, Kathy Brezinski-Stein, JoAnne Brockway, Jean Cole, Judith K. Coryell, Nancy Crewe, Cheryl Davis, Nancy Erikson, Walda Katz

Fishman, John Freal, Lex Frieden, Jan Fritz, Margaret Gardner, Lesley Hoyt, Mary Ann Lamana, Jerry Lorenz, Scott Manley, Susan Martina, Bernie Mermis, Sheila Miller, Hyman Miriam-Polaski, Helen Moore, Marcia Pavlov, Judy Plaskow, Constantina Safilios-Rothschild, Mary Kay Schleiter, Lois Schwab, Susan Shaul, Joanne Taggie, Dorothy Walters, Harold Wilke, Beatrice Wright, Margaret Zahn, and Irving Zola.

We also want to acknowledge the many physically disabled women we have known and who have supported this project. Their lives have been the source of our understanding not only the problems but also the strengths and stamina of physically disabled women. We hope that they are pleased with the book, as we are.

Mary Jo Deegan would like to acknowledge the help of her physical therapist, Marjorie Stamm, who taught her how to walk again and, more importantly, how to cope with the trauma of an adult disability. Odin Anderson has been a mainstay for her studies of disability and supported her personally and financially during her doctoral training in medical sociology. Michael R. Hill has patiently supported the work of editing by a calm presence and unflagging help at crucial periods.

Nancy Brooks acknowledges the sustaining energy of her husband, John, who walks a narrow line between helping her deal with multiple sclerosis and recognizing her need to cope independently. Irving Zola has been a role model in disability studies, and Dean Paul Magelli has provided a sensitive ear and financial support for professional development.

Finally, we would like to note that this book has allowed both editors to analyze an area intrinsic to our professional and personal lives. It has provided us the opportunity to grow as sociologists and as friends. It is our cooperation that has made this final product possible.

1

Introduction

Women and Disability: The Double Handicap

Mary Jo Deegan and Nancy A. Brooks

During the 1970s a social movement arose to address the concerns of people with disabilities. Action groups pressed for reforms in architectural barriers, educational and employment opportunities, deinstitutionalization, and legal protection of civil rights. Although accurate demographic information is lacking, estimates indicate that approximately one in ten Americans has a disability or chronic disease and would be directly affected by the disability movement. These people experience serious limitations in major activities such as housework, employment, or education. Although physical restrictions pose significant problems, social restrictions generated by negative attitudes impose greater handicaps, because socially created barriers effectively prevent full community participation. The primary purpose of the disability movement therefore has been to combat both environmental and social handicaps through public education and legal advances.

Despite the attention given to disability in general and certain impairments in particular, one category within the disabled population has received little recognition or study: women. Like many social change movements, the disability movement has often directed its energies toward primarily male experiences. Male sexual concerns and employment issues, for example, have received more attention than child-bearing problems. Our purpose here is to identify the issues and experiences that are particular to disabled women.

1

A Brief Note on the Collection of Essays

The papers assembled here are ample documentation of the special barriers to and strengths of physically disabled women. Each essay starts with a short abstract, allowing the reader to grasp the central points quickly. Each of these summaries introduces the individual paper far better than we can do in a traditional editorial review. We have chosen, instead, to present our response to the papers as a collection and to reflect on their implications as a set of writings.

These papers do have coherence, despite the variety and range of viewpoints included. The major factors unifying the collection are a central focus on the "double" jeopardy of disabled women, the lack of information available about their lives and experiences, and the need to alleviate the conditions that perpetuate structured inequality.

Fine and Asch have conceptualized the disabled woman as "roleless." In so doing, they point to the need for idealized social models, systematic recognition of social worth, and the enactment of abstract ideas of social placement within actual lives. Negative and delimiting stereotypes make disabled women a social category that is demeaned across situations and time. Nontraditional choices, such as never being married or being childless, can be interpreted as a function of narrow expectations, as an "inability" to achieve traditional roles instead of an independent choice of great meaning and commitment.

Deaf women, often living in institutional settings in their youth and separated from parents who cannot use sign language, are frequently more conservative than other women. Becker and Jauregui explain eloquently and insightfully that the social world is based on communication. Deafness can raise communication barriers which delay socialization and isolate the individual. By defining deafness as more than a hearing loss, they explain the underlying problem of deafness as a socially created barrier to understanding and participation. Social meaning and its nuances are conveyed through interaction, causing systematic limits on social intercourse for the hearing impaired. American Sign Language (ASL) is seen by many as the most viable communication system for the deaf, while many others dispute its value. One of the ways to help resolve this controversy would be a close analysis of the social meaning and interaction patterns that result from its use.

These types of social restrictions in daily living and in structured opportunities are not always clearly understood, by others or the women involved. The degree of consciousness of structured discrimination, as a woman and as a disabled person, is a necessary component of being a member of a minority group. "Multiple minority groups" must have both objective limitations on their participation in everyday life and a consciousness of their groups' restrictions. Deegan discusses the ramifications which follow the combination of more than one minority status. The articles in this volume reaffirm and document many of her points. Instances of discrimination by "liberated women" and by peer disabled men are dispersed throughout the collection of articles. Similarly, the courage and stamina of disabled women reveal their strengths and transcendence of the limited expectations that frequently surround them. Thus, this book is a beginning step in unraveling the interaction between more than one minority status being held concomitantly by an individual and a group. A greater understanding of this distinctiveness and similarity with other disadvantaged groups will aid in building "communication" and "community building" skills so badly needed by minorities in general.

In Kutza's article, a dramatic documentation of the economic effects of multiple minority status is given. In a truly insightful argument, she reveals that government benefits for disabled persons are systematically based on a patriarchal conception of work. This male-dominant world view is operationalized through programs that are primarily tied to work histories in the marketplace. Labor in the home is ineligible for remuneration through government programs, so much of "women's work" is not technically considered "work" nor rewarded economically. Most women who receive benefits, therefore, receive them in the more stigmatizing and lower-paid category of "welfare" rather than "workers' compensation" for labor expended as a legitimated contribution to the community.

Similarly, Bonwich examines the problems of traumatic spinal cord injuries and sheds light on the potential for nontraditional sex roles to build new strengths out of a situation of severe role loss. Pointing to the dearth of information about disabled women's lives, she uses interviews to document the changing lives of women who have disabilities. The extreme disruption in interpersonal relationships, sexuality, and in child bearing and rearing strikes at the core of traditional female roles. Rural women, moreover, may face limited options in job opportunities and counseling. Despite these difficulties, however, the spinal cord injured women whom she interviewed show us some of the ways out of dark dilemmas often handled in isolation and with despair.

Although each of these first five articles is concerned with pragmatic issues, they also address abstract ideas and develop generalized concepts. The remaining four articles continue to analyze the experiences and opportunities of disabled women but do so in more specific contexts.

Two articles, Kolb's on assertiveness training and Saxton's on peer counseling, are excellent examples of the coordination of interests among all of the authors. The early articles emphasized the need for disabled women to be active in the process of social change, then Kolb and Saxton provide us with information and reflection on two models of successful self-help programs.

Although all women are unjustifiably expected to be patient, passive and tranquil, the techniques for learning to be more assertive may be particularly difficult for a disabled woman to utilize. Advice on how to obtain one's rights may be based on the assumption that the woman is able-bodied. For example, Kolb discusses the problem of being unable to use eye contact as a mechanism to assert authority. This specific example reveals tellingly the more general problem of assertiveness for disabled women. The problems here may involve learning to be assertive, disregarding advice drawn from able-bodied women, and creating new ways to be assertive with limited physical capacities. In other words, disabled women must be assertive before they can follow traditional advice on how to be assertive! Kolb and her informants do provide us with some specific mechanisms for dealing with this issue, but their raising the general question is a particularly astute and valuable contribution. We have only begun to examine this crucial problem here. For example, to pose a more complicated problem for the reader, how can a deaf person who is limited in communication skills and nuances of interaction, as documented by Becker and Jauregui, confront a rude salesperson?

One answer to these dilemmas is peer counseling. Legitimated experience, shared trust, and knowledge-building are all possible benefits of meeting regularly and discussing systematically the lived reality of being both disabled and female. A twelve-week program of topics for such a group is presented by Saxton, and one group's response to this agenda illustrates its timeliness and significance. An emphasis on social action and change is important for making peer groups do more than engage in narcissistic analysis. The parallels with "consciousness-raising" groups are striking. Heightened awareness can uncover, discover, and recover a unity that generates power and identity. Peer counseling and assertiveness training, then, are two concrete methods to generate roles for disabled women, ending the present problems of rolelessness documented by Fine and Asch.

Eliminating the barriers to self-help is another way to resolve problems facing physically disabled women, and some of the most appalling barriers are those generated by the "helping" professions. Kutner and Gray document the lack of knowledge, understanding, and even denial of services associated with chronic renal failure in women. Dealing with a specific population, they provide systematic documentation of callousness in research and services and reveal the heretofore unknown linkage between being a woman and having this disability. Although they pinpoint a specific group, their work highlights the general, pervasive problems of (1) sexuality and the disabled woman, (2) the link between financial resources and receipt of services, and (3) the general lack of appreciation for or understanding of women's work in the home.

These same issues are discussed in very different settings in the remaining articles. McCharen and Earp have developed a complex model of employment practices for women with breast cancer. They show that formal knowledge about the disease is not sufficient to change the present situation of inequality. Emotional reactions to the stigma of disability and past experiences with the illness are prime motivating factors for employers that limit the effectiveness of "rational" information.

One interpretation of their findings leads to the vocational advice to encourage women with breast cancer to look at larger-sized organizations that have maximum sick leave policies and medical coverage. Although this is a short-term response to a serious problem in the marketplace, temporary aid is often vital. More research carefully explaining the variety of factors occurring in any one situation is badly needed. McCharen and Earp provide an excellent model for conducting further studies in this vein.

Finally, the last article by Shaul, Dowling, and Laden is on motherhood. There is a reason for ending the book with this chapter. The women who became mothers are so full of vitality, so positive about their choices, and so eloquent in their analysis that they provide a living example of both the stresses on and strengths of disabled women. Liberation involves taking risks and affirming life. Although motherhood has often been an oppressive status, glorifying self-negation and "saintliness," it has also been a positive opportunity for intimacy, regeneration, and human commitment. These disabled mothers have revealed the latter process and potential. In doing so, they provide us with lessons on what it is to create and challenge not only themselves, but also their children.

This last article is an excellent ending for what must be, by necessity, a rather grim set of readings. The lives of disabled women are severely limited in American society. Since this is the reality, it must be reflected here. In many ways, these papers are an indictment of a socially created world. Calls for more research, knowledge, and understanding must be heard in a world that is now economically distressed as well as "deaf," "immobile," "blind," and "paralyzed". It is society that is disabled, not our sisters who suffer from the social restrictions created by a handicapped symbolic and mythic world.

2

Disabled Women: Sexism without the Pedestal

Michelle Fine and Adrienne Asch

There is presently a dearth of information on the status of disabled women in U. S. society. In this paper we present an introductory statement on the lives of disabled women by delineating the economic, social and psychological constraints which place them at a distinct disadvantage relative to disabled men and nondisabled women. We begin by evaluating the ways in which a disability is viewed as an impediment to traditional and nontraditional sex role development. We then examine the profile of the disabled woman, propose a theoretical explanation of her imposed rolelessness, and recommend specific steps to ameliorate some of her role problems.

Introduction

It is estimated that 36 million persons in the U.S. have disabling conditions (Bowe, 1980). From another perspective, it is noted that 13,110,000 persons ages 16 to 64 have work disabilities: 8.5 percent of all working age females and 9.3 percent of all working age males (U.S. Bureau of Census, 1983). These figures alone, however, tell only a partial story. We argue here that disability is a more severely handicapping condition for women than for men.

We trace this differential experience to the more limited role choices and limited role models available to disabled women. Whereas disabled men are obliged to fight the social stigma of disability, they can aspire to fill socially powerful male roles. Disabled women do not have this option. Disabled women are perceived as inadequate for economically productive roles (traditionally considered appropriate for males) and for the nurturant, reproductive roles considered appropriate for females (Broverman, Clarkson and Rosenkrantz, 1972).

Examining the Context

The lack of approved adult social roles for disabled women derives from a constellation of confounding forces. Disabled women (like racial or ethnic minority women) experience a major disadvantage in relation to their relevant "single" minority reference groups: disabled men and non-disabled women (Harrison, 1977). The disadvantage is "double" because disabled women fare worse than both relevant comparison groups economically, socially, and psychologically.[1] These multiple dimensions of disadvantage are discussed in more depth below.

Economic Realities

Disabled women confront grim economic realities. The situation is even worse for racial/ethnic minorities within this population (Glover et al., 1979; Greenblum, 1977; Medvene and Akabas, 1979). It is estimated that between 65 percent and 76 percent of all disabled women are unemployed. During times of economic crisis, the economic status of this class cannot be expected to improve (O'Toole and Weeks, 1978; Rehab Group, 1979).

Unemployment problems are compounded by inequities in training programs. Disabled men are more likely than disabled women to be referred to vocational school or on-the-job training. While 94 percent of disabled men who are rehabilitated receive training in wage-earning occupations, only 68 percent of the disabled women are so trained (cf. O'Toole and Weeks, 1978).

Census and survey data consistently document the many problems facing disabled women: disabled women (1) are less likely to be employed than disabled men, (2) somewhat less likely to be college educated, and (3) earn substantially less (for vocationally rehabilitated men vs. women, the mean annual incomes are $4188 vs. $2744, respectively, Greenblum, 1977). Women are less likely to find a job post disability and those who do find a job are more likely to absorb a cut in pay. They are even more likely to live in families with incomes at or below the poverty level (Medvene and Akabas, 1979, Rehab Group, 1979; Schechter, 1977). Concomitantly, disabled women have disproportionately lower levels of disability coverage and insurance benefits (Greenblum, 1977), conditions which deepen their economic disadvantage.[2]

Social Realities

In social interactions, which are related to economic factors, disabled women are again at a disadvantage. While marriage may not be a preferred status for an increasing number of women, it is a customary measure of social options and position. Compared to nondisabled women, disabled women are more likely to never marry, marry at a later age and, once married, to be divorced

(Franklin, 1977). Of those individuals who are married with partner absent, separated, divorced or widowed, more are disabled women than disabled men. Similarly, a greater percentage of female heads of household than male heads of household are disabled (Rehab Group, 1979). Evidence collected on problem drinkers documents this even more dramatically—90 percent of women alcoholics are left by their husbands; 10 percent of men alcoholics are left by their wives (National Council on Alcoholism, 1980). Anecdotes and statistics alike suggest that disabled women are more likely to be left alone than are disabled men.

Other social factors, including sexual and reproductive relationships, differentially affect disabled women. While empirical data are largely unavailable, a growing grapevine and media coverage indicate that disabled women are often advised by professionals not to bear children, and are more likely (within race and class groupings) to be threatened by or victims of involuntary sterilization than nondisabled women (Committee for Abortion Rights and Against Sterilization Abuse, 1979). Reproductive freedom, child custody and domestic violence are particular concerns for these women who are traditionally overlooked when "optimal" social programs are formulated.

Because public opinion assumes disabled women to be inappropriate as mothers or sexual beings (Safilios-Rothschild, 1977), relevant information, counseling, technology and research findings are lacking. Safilios-Rothschild notes, for example, that because coronary research is almost exclusively conducted with men, women heart attack victims who inquire about resumption of sexual activity are advised by physicians who use male-derived standards. More often than not, the women receive no answers at all. The social neglect of the sexual and reproductive roles of disabled women worsens the circumstances that they confront in personal relationships.

Psychological Realities

Disabled women, in self-perceptions and as perceived by others, are viewed more negatively than are disabled men. Disabled women report more negative self-images (Weinberg, 1976), are perceived in less favorable ways (cf. Miller, 1970), and are more likely to be a victim of hostility than are disabled men (Tilly and Viney, 1969). Self-concept research finds that negative self-concept is less related to one's level of ability/disability than to one's gender (Weinberg, 1976). Self-perceptions of these women conform to the perceptions expressed by others (Mead, 1934), and may unfortunately be an accurate internalization of opportunity structures.

Disabled women are not only more likely to internalize society's rejection, but they are also more likely than disabled men to identify themselves as "disabled". The disabled male possesses a relatively positive self-image, and is more likely to identify as "male" rather than as "disabled". The disabled woman appears more likely to introject society's rejection, and to identify as "disabled" (Dailey, 1979; Meissner, Thoreson and Butler, 1967; Weinberg, 1976). In research conducted by Mauer (1979), disabled females were more likely than disabled males to identify with a disabled storybook character, while the disabled males were more likely to identify with the nondisabled character. Disabled men may have a choice between a role of advantage (male) and a role of disadvantage (disability). Their decision is frequently a strategic identification with males.

The combined forces of a hostile economy, a discriminatory society, and negative self-image contribute to a systematic *rolelessness* for disabled women. There is no avenue for self-affirmation.

Perspectives and Responses

Prior to the passage of the Rehabilitation Act of 1973, many people thought of the disabled population as limited to obvious examples such as the deaf, the blind, the orthopedically impaired, and the mentally retarded. Now, the federal government has defined "disability" to include persons who have or who are regarded as having a limitation or interference with daily life activities such as hearing, speaking, seeing, walking, moving, thinking, breathing, and learning (Pub. L. 93-122, Pub. L. 95-602). The disabled population entitled to rehabilitation services and to protection against discrimination in employment and education includes persons with invisible impairments such as those with arthritis, diabetes, epilepsy, heart and respiratory problems, cancer, and developmental disabilities such as mental retardation, psychiatric disorders, substance abuse, or obesity. This population experiences great diversity in their day-to-day problems. Some persons, such as those who are disfigured or obese, may have no actual limitations on physical activity, but are regarded as potentially restricted due to their physical presentation. Others, by employing a range of alternative techniques, carry on in all manners of daily life activities in spite of the inability to walk, speak, see or hear. The very methods of defining disability may confuse the problems intrinsic to a health condition with those arising from attitudinal, institutional, environmental, and legal barriers that are socially constructed and maintained.

For the purposes of this article, we are considering the situation of that disabled girl or young woman who becomes disabled with a severe impairment of vision, hearing, mobility, or body structure (such as loss or deformity of an arm or leg) before defining herself vocationally or socially. We recognize that this represents only a portion of the total population, but we suggest that examining her situation best illustrates the difficulties of all disabled women.

Stereotypes and Roles

> . . . the satisfied fervour of one who has at last pinned a label on a rare specimen: "She is, of course, one of your typical English spinsters . . . I suppose she has given up?" "Given up what?" I asked (Lessing, 1963: 188).

A social role involves those behaviors which an individual in a particular situation engages, based on the normative demands and/or the expectations of others (Merton, 1968; Goffman, 1973). A role set is that configuration of social relations in which an individual is involved because of his/her social position(s); e.g., daughter, wife, manager, therapist (Merton, 1967). From this constellation, people move in an out of roles. Roles are, for the most part, situationally determined. We argue here that women with disabilities have been offered no socially sanctioned roles.

Stereotypes, on the other hand, are those behaviors expected from an individual by virtue of a stable characteristic (e.g., disabled women) (Sennett, 1977). People are often perceived as a function of a single, salient characteristic. Then, a composite of characteristics associated with that one characteristic are stereotypically attributed to the individual. Stereotypes help perceivers order the world and prepare for predictable interactions (Goffman, 1973), but stereotypes can be both narrow and inaccurate.

Roles shift with situations; stereotypes persist across situations. Stereotypes function to constrain the number and diversity of roles which women can appropriately fill. While this tendency is changing for women in general (Locksley, Borgida, Brekke and Hepburn, 1980), disabled women still are viewed primarily through rigid, constraining stereotypes (cf. Anderson, Lepper and Ross, 1980).

Caricatured profiles of women and of the disabled do reflect some economic, social and psychological realities. Frequently, however, they also perpetuate and justify the most unfair aspects of these realities (Kanter, 1977). To illustrate the tautology of stereotypes, consider the presumption that "A disabled woman needs a man to take care of her; if she can find one" (New York Governor's Conference on Families: Session on Disabled Women, 1980). While a disabled woman may *choose* to enter a relationship with a man, the extent to which she *needs* to do so may result only from the fact that a woman's social and economic status still derives largely from her relationship with a man. Disabled women generally receive inadequate training for personal and professional self-sufficiency and suffer the brunt of labor force discrimination. As a class, disabled women are consequently less able to earn living wages. Tautologically, these women may need a man largely because the stereotypes justify and self-fulfill an unfair reality (Merton, 1968).

While men and women, disabled or not, fall prey to many stereotypes, disabled men and disabled women have varying access to distinct social roles. Disabled men may perceive a choice between two relatively incongruous roles—being male and being disabled. Disabled women may perceive a choice between two more congruous roles—being female and being disabled. To be a male in our society is to be strong, assertive, and independent; to be female is to be weak, passive, and dependent (Broverman et al., 1972; La France and Mayo, 1979), the latter conforming to the social stereotype of the disabled (Schroedel, 1978). From both categories the disabled woman inherits ascriptions of weakness and passivity (Baker and Reitz, 1978).

During the past decade, however, men and women have increasingly rejected traditionally rigid sex roles. If men were expected to be wage earners and women homemakers/mothers (Komarovsky, 1946; O'Leary, 1977), today both are exploring alternatives. While sex-role ambiguity continues to complicate (if liberate) the lives of the nondisabled (cf. Horner, 1972), the disabled woman is still viewed as unable to fulfill either adult role—that of wage-earner or that of homemaker.

Disability: A Predominant Characteristic

Being disabled is a characteristic sufficient to stereotype an individual. Therefore disabled men and women are viewed, and often come to view themselves, as primarily disabled. This occurs if the person was born disabled or acquires a disability later (Scott, 1969). The nondisabled world is structured so that disability often becomes the predominant characteristic by which a person is labeled.

To illustrate this point, let us examine how national statistics on the prevalence of disability have been gathered. Organizations such as the Social Security Administration and the U.S. Census, in order to estimate the numbers of disabled persons, ask people about their "limitations" in addition to their health conditions. In order to distinguish a "disorder", which would be a physiological/psychological deviation from the "norm", an "impairment" which involves limitation of individuals to perform specific tasks, and a "handicap" which involves limited social functioning of an individual, distinct questions need to be asked (cf. Peterson, Lowman, and Kirchner, 1978). Often questions are phrased in such a way that health status is linked to limitations in kinds or amounts of work or activities to be performed, rather than simply asking if there are health problems. Many severely disabled persons who, because of quadriplegia, deafness or blindness, require attendants, interpreters, readers, and/or other technological and social resources to function successfully, refuse to answer "yes" to any questions that would categorize them as "impaired" or "handicapped" in spite of their obvious necessity for assistance to overcome physical limitations. Furthermore, those respondents who do answer "yes" may be accurately reflecting discrimination they have encountered, fears they may have in seeking employment, or the realistic inaccessibility of transit systems, office buildings, and housing. The problem, in short, remains: when a "disorder" is recognized, a "handicap" is assumed.

The label of disability carries with it such a powerful imputation of inability to perform any adult social function that there is no other descriptor needed by the public (Gliedman and Roth, 1980; Lukoff, 1960). The exception to our assertion that disabled people are viewed myopically is the successful disabled person. He or she is not considered an exception but rather is remembered for performing some function well, and not for doing that while disabled. Gliedman and Roth contrast the legacies of Beethoven, Milton, Franklin Delano Roosevelt and Julius Caesar (all disabled, by the way, in midlife and postsuccess) with the ways in which black successes are conceptualized. The outstanding black person is viewed as both successful and black, reminding minority and majority persons that there are exceptions to the generally devalued status of the black person in the U.S. The outstanding disabled person (i.e. male) is viewed as successful but not as disabled.

One might take issue with Gliedman and Roth's notion that the blackness of Paul Robeson or James Baldwin enhances the public view of blacks. Nevertheless, the crucial point is that the disabled person, as conceived by the nondisabled world, has no abilities or social functions. Those who do perform successfully are no longer viewed as disabled.

Writings by disabled women themselves bear out the dominance of disability in their own self-definitions. A black disabled woman writes, "Of the three minorities of which I am a member, the handicap has dominated my life" (O'Toole and Weeks, 1978). In the absence of data, we speculate that the reason for this statement stems from the dominance that this characteristic assumed in her family—a dominance assumed to be present in the family of every disabled child who grows up with nondisabled parents imbued with a profound fear of disability (Featherstone, 1980).

Rolelessness: The Outcome

Rolelessness, the absence of sanctioned social roles and/or institutional means to achieve these roles, characterizes the circumstances of disabled women in today's society (Merton, 1967). While it may sound like a blessing to have no socially prescribed roles to reject, in actuality to have no roles to aspire toward, internalize, or reject is likely to be costly. The absence of sanctioned roles can cultivate a psychological sense of invisibility (O'Toole and Weeks, 1978), self-estrangement, and/or powerlessness (Blauner, 1964).

Without roles to adopt or reject, and without role models to emulate or deviate from, disabled girls grow up feeling not just different but inferior. While we recognize that role models alone would not solve the problem, the absence of role models and sanctioned roles may introduce feelings of worthlessness which complicate disability. For example, a study of disabled adults indicates that a full 20% of the respondents volunteered the fact that they make social comparisons to *no one*. They have no basis on which to appraise their own abilities or achievements (Strauss, 1968). Disabled girls may find themselves unable to estimate their actual abilities or speculate on realistic aspirations. Nondisabled parents, siblings, and teachers discourage these girls from using nondisabled role models because these authority figures, like many others, believe that the disability is the most salient and defining characteristic of that child.

Trapped in two socially devalued roles, disabled women, not surprisingly, subscribe to more traditional notions of femininity than do nondisabled women (Cook and Rossett, 1975). Why this is true is left to speculation. It may be difficult to reject a role which you have never had. The "costs" of sexist remarks, unpleasant harassment, and sexual objectification may be less apparent to disabled women who have been more the victims of social (e.g., male) neglect. One woman, disabled from birth and a feminist, commented at the New York Governor's Conference on Families (1980), "Though I'd probably hate it, I don't know what it's like to be whistled at on the street". To be denied the opportunity to fulfill the social role prescribed for women may make the role more appealing (or less unappealing) to disabled women (Brehmn, 1966). To be perceived as attractive, nurturant, and supportive by men, the women must overcome routine neglect and/or hostility from nondisabled men (Titley and Viney, 1969). Men express more negative stereotypes of disability, have less contact with disabled individuals, and are more likely to exhibit hostility to disabled individuals than are non-disabled women (Gottlieb and Corman, 1975; Higgs, 1975; Titley and Viney, 1979; Smith and McCulloch, 1978). Such dynamics frustrate heterosexual disabled women in attempts to fulfill the traditional "feminine" role.

Contrary to women's perceptions of what men want in an "ideal mate", men report that their "ideal mate" should be assertive and independent (Steinmann and Fox, 1974). This may explain the documented hostility of nondisabled men toward disabled women (Titley and Viney, 1969) whom they view as hyperdependent. Clearly, this dynamic is an important area for future research.

Rolelessness may induce high dependence on external forces for self-definition. Rival theories about sex role development, formulated by Bandura and Kohlberg, offer perspectives on the ways in which little girls come to identify "female". Bandura (1969) suggests that children imitate like role models so that girl children pattern themselves after their mothers and other adult women. Kohlberg (1966) offers a more cognitive classification system in which children learn "I am a girl" and then adopt appropriate attitudes and behaviors. Because disabled girls are viewed first as disabled, their parents may not know which to adopt. If this formulation of the situation is correct, disabled girls may internalize expectations established for girls through the media, television, teachers, school books, etc. (Gillespie and Fink, 1974) and fall prey to a set of influences that devalue female roles. In the absence of countervailing forces—such as supportive parents, teachers, or significant others—disabled women may be more likely than nondisabled women to assimilate traditional notions of their "place" in society (Cook and Rosset, 1975). With whom disabled girls identify raises another significant area of research.

The absence of social roles for disabled women is a handicapping condition. It is likely to limit career and personal options, hinder full development, and obstruct free choices. The labor market, family attitudes, and sexism in schools reinforce these limitations. We have argued that for men and women with disabilities, disability stereotypes and the "disability" role dominate their lives. Yet we are presented with the interesting fact that for men, disabled and nondisabled, their self-concept is reported to be better than that of women, disabled and nondisabled (Weinberg, 1976). The male sex role is more valued than the female sex role in America (McKee and Sherifs, 1957). In this light, one may not be surprised by this finding. However, the fact that disabled men have better self-image than nondisabled women is puzzling (Weinberg, 1976). If we can believe this finding, we propose that disabled men, if they figure out how to adopt the male characteristics of assertiveness, independence, and pro-activity, can get an "edge" on the disability that is unavailable to disabled women. By refining their adeptness at the "male" role they can escape some restrictions of the "disability" role. Such an escape hatch is unavailable to disabled women. Perfecting the female sex role only reinforces the stereotypic, passive disability role.

Disabled men have mentioned another strategy by which they escape some of the traditional role-baggage associated with being disabled. In a study of successful disabled scientists, respondents were asked to indicate effective coping strategies. Frequently, the male respondents noted that their wives helped them manage, instrumentally and affectively, their personal and professional endeavors (Redden, personal communication, 1978). Disabled women, as we well know, have no wives. For years, nondisabled women have expressed the need for a "wife" (Syfers, 1973). Because women's success in the past has been defined primarily as deriving from marital rather than occupational status, many women have come to view themselves successful if chosen by men. As we have noted, disabled women are less likely to have this "privilege". They are therefore less likely to be socially defined as having and filing the "women's role", and less likely to feel personally successful. The fact that disabled women are more likely to be without a spouse limits, relatively, the extent of personal and professional support they can expect.

A Critical Review

In this paper we have taken the position that disabled women suffer economically, socially and psychologically more than their disabled male and nondisabled female counterparts. While we acknowledge that disability is costly for men and women, we argue that the latter bear the brunt of double discrimination.

The reader should be cautious of such assertions. It is far too easy to pity the disabled woman-as-victim, and to feed the helpless stereotype we have just critiqued. We would like, therefore, to qualify our perspective with a reminder that we do view disabled women as victims of economic, social and psychological forces but that we see disabled women as neither helpless nor hopeless victims unwilling to change their circumstances. Many disabled women are in fact emerging as traditional successes in professional and personal endeavors. Others are even making untraditional choices, breaking out of the confines of their gender-specific and their disability-specific constraints. But, there is, again, a catch when disabled women challenge long-adhered-to stereotypes.

More and more, during the last 15 years, nondisabled women have challenged their traditional options, and created new ones. Single motherhood, professionalism, nontraditional careers, and lifestyle choices allow many women to justify to themselves and to the world that they have made a choice (recognizing, of course, economic and social constraints). To justify a nontraditional *choice* is more difficult for disabled women. The disabled woman who chooses to be a lesbian, opts to be a successful professional, or assumes an assertive, independent lifestyle may be viewed as having made these decisions of necessity rather than of choice. Again, the predominant characteristic looms large. In this perspective, the disabled woman is perceived as a disability-determined entity: lifestyles, sexual preference, and personal decisions are viewed as consequences of the disability rather than choices.

While economic and social conditions do impede choices for all women, and many disabled women are placed in circumstances which they would not choose, to perceive all decisions of disabled women as disability-determined is a dangerous presumption. If disabled women subscribe to the notion of limited potential choices, if they accept the consequences of discrimination and view all outcomes as independent of their own actions, a sense of helplessness may evolve (Seligman, 1975). The woman who sees herself as a hopeless victim may be oblivious to the potential for collective options that could be developed, and to the injustice around her (Fine, M., 1979). While the unjust economic and social realities need to be confronted, the extent to which they have been, or will continue to be, entirely limiting needs to be questioned.

In light of these social psychological observations, a rapidly changing legislative policy toward the disabled, the long-awaited incorporation of disabled women into the women's movement, and the more general visibility of disabled women, many institutional ramifications are pertinent.

Implications

The theoretical focus of this essay has been on the rolelessness imposed upon disabled women. The data we have presented are derived from survey materials and literature reviews. Integration of these materials allows us the opportunity to glance at what the "facts" say—slim as they are—and to identify the implications of these concerns. We are aware that many of the implications to be noted are appropriate to disabled men as well as disabled women. Some of the concerns are specific to women, however, and others have more impact on women. These receive particular attention below.

Economic Implications

In recent years there have been legislative mandates to hire the disabled, to create accessible structures and to provide adequate benefits to disabled individuals. While legislative and judicial activity is critical, these accomplishments alone are insufficient to improve substantially the living standards of the disabled population. A complementary way to effect change economically is through grass roots political activity. The potential for change in this arena is enormous.

Disabled women are coming out: they are beginning to examine their issues publicly, forcing other groups to address their issues politically, and are organizing (Kitsousa, 1980). The book in which this chapter appears is evidence of a long-closeted private trouble becoming a public issue. The most apparent aspect of this public emergence is within the women's movement and within the disability movement. Ironically, it is within these movements that the distinct role and (rolelessness) of the disabled woman is most clear. Although there certainly are prominent exceptions, most disabled activist women would agree that males obtain most of the leadership positions within groups of disabled persons. Disabled women activists have voiced the view that at meetings with disabled males they are expected to carry out traditional female roles of taking minutes or serving food and are expected to let the men dominate as spokespersons (Women's Caucus of the White House Conference of Handicapped Individuals, personal communications, n.d.). Others note the reluctance with which the women's movement has incorporated a disability perspective. Both movements have been conservative in recognizing or in supporting the issues unique to disabled women.

For disabled women to organize as a political unit, they must achieve both differentiation and integration (Katz and Katz, 1978). As a political strategy, the women need to differentiate their issues, needs, demands, and rights as distinct from those of disabled men and nondisabled women. Concomitantly, to mobilize resources effectively and to broaden their social roles, it is politically advantageous for disabled women to integrate with other political groups—women, ethnic minorities, labor, etc. To encourage economic changes, disabled women must come to view their circumstances as politically and economically influenced. They must then educate others about the economic roots of the conditions faced by most disabled women, while they align with other political groups struggling with similar issues.

Social Implications

To increase the range and number of roles available to disabled women, new roles and role models must be made available. Key figures for instituting these changes are already working in the social services, medicine, and education. Services for parents are of the utmost importance: information guides, counseling, or self-help groups may be critical to the healthy development of disabled children and the healthy development of a society which integrates rather than isolates its disabled members (Featherstone, 1980). Child advocates can help parents interact forcefully and efficiently with relevant institutions (Brown, 1979).

Training for teachers is also critical. With the implementation of mainstreaming, many teachers work with disabled children and are under-equipped to respond effectively. In the absence of appropriate information, the teachers may overprotect, neglect, and/or transmit negative messages to the disabled child. Vocational rehabilitation counselors and employers also need to understand that disability and gender do not necessarily interfere with work performance.

The child custody, reproductive freedom, and domestic violence movements also need to encompass the concerns of disabled women. For example, battered women's shelters which are not accessible to the disabled, or are not advertised as accessible, can do a disservice to battered disabled women. While we argue that disabled women need to reach out to many activist groups, this linking needs to be reciprocal.

Psychological Implications

Many of the psychological issues which trouble disabled women can be alleviated by parents, teachers, and employers who are supportive and encouraging of these young women. Nonetheless, other problems are likely to persist. Most important, the socio-genesis of these problems needs to be understood by the disabled women (and men) and by mental health practitioners who work with disabled individuals. Living in an unsupportive social environment, often without a job, can be psychologically unhealthy. Poor self-image, a sense of rejection, or awkwardness is a reasonable response to such social treatment, or rolelessness.

To provide support to disabled women, therapeutic and/or support groups could be organized so that the women do not—as women tend to do—internalize their problems and identify them as individual rather than social. These groups can provide information as well as support. Similarly, involving disabled women in heterogeneous women's groups is important. While it is tempting to organize disabled women's groups, and disabled mother's groups, etc., it is dangerous to overidentify the disabilities and ignore the whole women.

Research Questions

It has been presumed here that disabled men have access to many of the role models and resources available to men, while even the traditional place preserved for women—that of wife/mother/sexual being—is withheld from disabled women. Accordingly, these women suffer what we have considered *rolelessness*. We suggest that attitudes and behaviors of parents, teachers, employers, potential social partners, and the disabled women themselves contribute to the situation of rolelessness. Below are eight categories of research appropriate for examining the extent and impact of rolelessness among disabled women.

1. Who are the role models identified by disabled girls (vs. disabled boys)? To whom do they self-compare; to whom do they aspire? To what extent do these girls (relative to disabled boys and nondisabled girls) perceive limited opportunities to fulfill personal and/or professional aspirations?
2. To what extent do parents contribute to differing aspirations, opportunities and role models for disabled boys and girls? How do the parents of boys vs. girls envision their children's futures? How do they prepare the children for these futures?
3. What balance of self-identification with women, with disabled others, and/or with disabled women maximizes the opportunities for a disabled girl/young woman to develop a self-image which incorporates, but does not deny nor allow dominance by, the disability?
4. How do personal and professional aspirations of disabled girls evolve over the years? At what point (if any) do they begin to conform to stereotypic

expectations? What paths are pursued? What are the barriers—internal and external—to realizing the original aspirations?

5. How do school teachers, rehabilitation counselors, and educational materials deal with disability for girls and boys? To what extent do schools offer sex education that considers the disabled? How is mainstreaming perceived by the children, the teachers, and the parents?

6. To what cause do disabled women (vs. men) attribute personal difficulties? Are disabled women more likely than disabled men to attribute personal and professional difficulties to self, rather than to other external factors? To what extent do mental health practitioners, counselors, employers, etc. collude in this self-blame rather than understand the social circumstances which create Catch-22s for disabled women?

7. Under what conditions is it possible for some disabled women to put disability back into their lives and affirm themselves as people who have rights, while disabled, to first-class citizenship? What permits some people to be successful without denying, hiding, or escaping from their disabilities?

8. To what extent does rolelessness characterize the situation of the woman who becomes disabled during adulthood? Is rolelessness mediated by marital status, work-force level, or participation, or status as a parent?

9. Research on the physical impact of disability on women (cf. Safilios-Rothschild's comment about the female heart attack victim) and its social psychological impact needs to be conducted. If disabled women are to develop heterogeneous and socially valued self-images, they require a foundation of substantial evidence and alternatives.

Conclusions

We argue in this article that the position of the disabled woman is inextricably linked with the socio-economic processes that define the positions of disabled men and nondisabled women. The devalued roles of nondisabled women and disabled men differ from the rolelessness experienced by disabled women in the United States. Disabled women confront the sexism experienced by most women, but are deprived of even the fragile pedestal on which nondisabled women are often placed. Research, political action, and altered social consciousness will provide the springboards for change.

Notes

The authors wish to acknowledge the invaluable contributions of Corinne Kirchner to this chapter.

1. For a discussion of this multiple effect, see Deegan, Chapter 4, in this volume.
2. For a documentation of different government benefits, see Kutza, Chapter 6, in this volume.

References

Anderson, C., H. Lepper, and L. Ross. 1980. "Perseverance of social theories: The role of explanation in the persistence of discredited information." *Journal of Personality and Social Psychology* 39: 1037-50.

Baker, L. and H. Reitz. 1978. "Altruism toward the blind: Effects of sex of helper and dependence of victim." *Journal of Social Psychology* 104: 19-28.

Bandura, A. 1969 "Social learning theory and identification processes." In D. Goslin, ed. *Handbook of Socialization Theory and Research*. Chicago: Rand McNally. Pp. 213-62.

Bem, S. 1975. "Sex role adaptability: One consequence of psychological androgyny." *Journal of Personality and Social Psychology* 31: 634-43.

Blauner, R. 1964. *Alienation and Freedom*. Chicago: University of Chicago Press.

Bowe, F. 1980. *Rehabilitating America*. New York: Harper and Row.

Brehm, J. 1966. *A Theory of Psychological Reactance*. New York: Academic Press.

Broverman, I., S. Vogel, D. Broverman, F. Clarkson and S. Rosenkrantz. 1972. "Sex-role stereotypes: A current appraisal." *Journal of Social Issues* 28: 59-78.

Brown, S. 1979. "Assuring due process in special educational placement and the roles of child and youth service professionals." *Child and Youth Services* 2: 1, 3-11.

Committee for Abortion Rights and Against Sterilization Abuse. 1979. *Women Under Attack: Abortion, Sterilization Abuse and Reproductive Freedom*. New York.

Cook, L. and A. Rossett. 1975. "The sex role attitudes of deaf adolescent women and their implications for vocational choice." *American Annals of the Deaf* 120: 341-45.

Dailey, A. 1979. "Physically handicapped women." *Counseling Psychologist* 8: 41-42.

Dodd, J. 1977. "Overcoming occupational stereotypes related to sex and deafness." *American Annals of the Deaf* 122:489-91.

Featherstone, H. 1980. *A Difference in the Family*. New York: Basic Books.

Fine, J. 1980. "Advice to parents from a disabled child." *American Rehabilitation* 5: 24-25.

Fine, M. 1979. "Options to injustice: Seeing other lights." *Representative Research in Social Psychology* 10: 61-76.

Franklin, P. 1977. "Impact of disability on the family structure." *Social Security Bulletin* 40: 3-18.

Gillespie, P. and A. Fink. 1974. "The influence of sexism on the education of handicapped children." *Exceptional Children* 5: 155-62.

Gliedman, J. and D. Roth. 1980. *The Unexpected Minority*. New York: Harcourt, Brace and Jovanovich.

Glover, R., P. Greenfield, A. King and P. Norval. 1979. *Stepping Up: Placing Minority Women into Managerial and Professional Jobs*. Salt Lake City, Utah: Olympus.

Goffman, E. 1963. *Stigma: Notes on the Management of Spoiled Identity*. Englewood Cliffs, N.J.: Prentice-Hall.

———. 1973. *The Presentation of Self in Everyday Life*. Woodstock, N.Y.: Overlook.

Gottlieb, J. and L. Corman. 1975. "Public attitudes to mentally retarded children." *American Journal of Mental Deficiency* 80: 72-80.

Greenblum, J. 1977. "Effect of vocational rehabilition on employment and earnings of the disabled." *Social Security Bulletin* 40: 3-16.

Harrison, A. 1977. "Black women." In V. O'Leary, ed. *Toward Understanding Women.* Monterey, Calif.: Brooks/Cole. Pp. 131-46.

Higgs, A. 1975. "Attitude formation—contact or information." *Exceptional Children* 41: 496-97.

Horner, M. 1972. "Toward an understanding of achievement-related conflicts in women." *Journal of Social Issues* 28: 157-76.

Hyman, H., J. Stokes and M. Strauss. 1973. "Occupational aspirations among the totally blind." *Social Forces* 51: 403-16.

Kanter, R. 1977. *Men and Women of the Corporation.* New York: Basic Books.

Katz, D. and R. Kahn. 1978. *The Social Psychology of Organizations.* New York: John Wiley and Sons.

Kitsousa, J. "Coming out all over." *Social Problems* 28: 1-11.

Kohlberg, L. 1966. "A cognitive developmental analysis of children's sex role concepts and attitudes." In E. Maccoby, ed. *The Development of Sex Differences.* Stanford, Calif.: Stanford University Press. Pp. 82-173.

Komarovsky, M. 1946. "Cultural contradictions and sex roles." *American Journal of Sociology* 52: 184-89.

La France, M. and C. Mayo. 1979. "A review of nonverbal behaviors of women and men." *Western Journal of Speech Communication* 43: 96-107.

Lessing, D. 1963. "Our Judith." In D. Lessing. *A Man and Two Women: Stories by Doris Lessing.* New York: Popular Library. Pp. 188-208.

Locksley, A., E. Borgida, N. Brekke, and C. Hepburn. 1980. "Sex stereotypes and social judgment." *Journal of Personality and Social Psychology* 39: 821-31.

Lukoff, I. 1960. "A sociological appraisal of blindness." In S. Finestone, ed. *Social Casework and Blindness.* New York: American Foundation for the Blind. Pp. 19-44.

Mauer, R. 1979. "Young children's response to a physically disabled storybook hero." *Exceptional Children* 45: 326-30.

McKee, J. and A. C. Sherifs. 1957. "The differential evaluation of males and females." *Journal of Personality* 25: 356-71.

Mead, G. H. 1934. *Mind, Self and Society.* Chicago: University of Chicago Press.

Medvene, L. and S. Akabas. 1979. *The Job Hunt of the Disabled.* New York: Industrial Social Welfare Center, Columbia University School of Social Work.

Meissner, A., R. Thoreson and A. Bultler. 1967. "Relation of self-concept to impact and obviousness of disability among male and female adolescents." *Perceptual and Motor Skills* 24: 1099-1105.

Merton, R. 1967. *On Theoretical Sociology.* New York: Free Press.

————.1968. *Social Theory and Social Structure.* Glencoe, Ill.: Free Press.

Miller, A. 1970. "Role of physical attractiveness in impression formation." *Psychonomic Science* 19: 241-43.

Myers, L. 1975. "Black women: Selectivity among roles and reference groups in the maintenance of self-esteem." *Journal of Social and Behavioral Sciences* 21: 39-47.

National Council on Alcoholism. 1980. *Facts on Alcoholism and Women.* New York: Affiliate.

New York Governor's Conference on Families, 1980.

O'Leary, V. 1977. *Toward Understanding Women.* Monterey, Calif: Brooks/Cole Publishing.

O'Toole, J. and C. Weeks. 1978. *What Happens After School? A Study of Disabled Women and Education.* San Francisco: Women's Educational Equity Communications Network.

Peterson, R., C. Lowman and C. Kirchner. 1978. "Visual handicap: Statistical data on a social process." *Visual Impairment and Blindness* 72: 419-21

Pub. L. 93-112, 87 Stat. 355. *Rehabilitation Act of 1973.*

Pub. L. 95-602, 92 Stat. 2955. *Rehabilitation Comprehension Services and Developmental Disabilities Amendments of 1978.*

Redden, M. 1978. American Association for the Advancement of Science. Personal Communication.

Rehab Group. 1979. *Digest of Data on Persons with Disabilities.* Falls Church, Va., May.

Safilios-Rothschild, C. 1977. "Discrimination against disabled women." *International Rehabilitation Review.* February: 4.

Schechter, E. 1977. "Employment and work adjustment of the disabled. *Social Security Bulletin* 40: 3-15.

Schroedel, J. 1978. *Attitudes Toward Persons with Disabilities.* New York: Human Resources Center.

Scott, R. A. 1969. *The Making of Blind Men: A study of Adult Socialization.* New York: Russell Sage Foundation.

Seligman, M. 1975. *Helplessness.* San Francisco: Freeman.

Sennett, R. 1977. *The Psychology of Society.* New York: Vintage Books.

Smith, N. and J. McCulloch. 1978. "Measuring attitudes toward the physically disabled." *International Journal of Rehabilitation Research* 1: 187-97.

Steinmen, A. and D. Fox. 1974. *The Male Dilemma.* New York: Aronson.

Strauss, H. 1968. "Reference group and social comparison processes among the totally blind." In H. Hyman and E. Singer, eds. *Readings in Reference Group Theory and Research.* New York: Free Press. Pp. 222-37.

Syfers, J. 1973. "Why I want a wife." In A. Koedt, E. Levine and A. Rapone, eds. *Radical Feminism.* New York: Quadrangle. Pp. 60-62.

Titley, R. and W. Viney. 1969. "Expression of aggression toward the physically handicapped." *Perceptual and Motor Skills* 29: 51-56.

U.S. Bureau of the Census. 1983. *Current Population Reports.* Series P-23, 127. Labor Force Status and Other Characteristics of Persons with a Work Disability. 1982. Washington, D.C.: U.S. Government Printing Office.

U.S. Department of Health, Education and Welfare. 1977. *Current Estimates from the Health Interview Survey.* Washington, D.C.: U.S. Government Printing Office.

Weinberg, N. 1976. "The effect of physical disability on self-perception." *Rehabilitation Counseling Bulletin.* September: 15-20.

Women's Caucus of the White House Conference of Handicapped Individuals. Personal Communication, n. d.

3

The Invisible Isolation of Deaf Women: Its Effect on Social Awareness

Gaylene Becker and Joanne K. Jauregui

The place of deaf women in relation to society is discussed, and the formative experiences that shape their personal development are described. Deaf women's needs are delineated, and suggestions are made for providers to meet these needs.

Introduction

In recent years, women's place in society has come under close scrutiny. The attention brought to bear on stereotypes and attitudes about women, their roles, and their relationships has created a climate in which social change is beginning to occur. In contrast, deaf women remain almost untouched by these changes. The deaf community reflects the most traditional and conservative attitudes that our society holds about women, attitudes that are perpetuated because deaf people are separated from the "hearing world" by the communication barrier created by deafness.

Methodology

The observations in this paper are based on the authors' experiences in the deaf community of the San Francisco Bay Area. Becker, a medical anthropologist, has conducted two one-year research projects on deaf persons. The first project, carried out with 200 deaf persons over the age of 60, was concerned with the impact of lifelong deafness on old age. Data were gathered through daily participant observation and through in-depth interviews with 60 persons. The second project was carried out with deaf persons between the ages of 20 and 60 and focused on adaptation to deafness over the life cycle, with particular attention to the development of coping behavior. In addition to extensive participant-observation in the deaf community, she carried out 40 in-depth interviews. She has also worked as a staff member and as a volunteer in various agencies that provide services to deaf people.

Jauregui, an educator and social service provider, taught deaf children and adolescents in special education programs for 16 years before she began to work with adults. Since 1978, she has coordinated a project that provides services (such as counseling, job development, the development of living skills, and advocacy) to deaf clients. In response to the needs she observed among her clients, she has developed educational programs for low-functioning deaf persons, sex education programs open to the entire deaf community, and has sponsored a variety of consciousness-raising activities for deaf women. She is an active participant in many aspects of deaf community life and is herself deaf.

Deafness: The Invisible Disability

> Emily Jones (pseudonym) screwed up her courage and walked through the senior center entrance. She was very lonely at home by herself and had been thinking of going to the Center for months. But it was a "hearing" agency, even though some of the staff knew sign language. She knew her visit might be a disaster. She dreaded making any mistakes. So she smiled warmly at the people at the front desk and walked quickly past them, not hearing them shout, "Come back back and sign in," or seeing them shake their heads at each other. She walked on until she saw an approachable-looking man with a cane. He smiled at her. She took out a pad of paper and wrote "Deaf?" on it. The man started to nod and tell her something. She did not understand him. Like most deaf people, she could not read lips. He seemed to realize this because he pointed, then he motioned her to go with him. She followed him through several rooms to a door that said, "Deaf Program." People were standing inside signing to each other. The man walked into the room and drew their attention to himself. He pointed to Emily. They all moved toward her with arms outstretched, smiling and talking all at once. She was very relieved.

The initial experience Emily Jones had in this agency was off to a good start. Deaf and hearing staff members who understood the potential pitfalls of the hearing world and who could communicate with her in sign language were there to help overcome the barriers that exist for a deaf person in a world that can hear. But even in such a benign setting, there are pitfalls that expose the deaf person to mortification and embarrassment.

> Later on that day Emily was given a membership application to fill out. She worked on this form by herself for a long time, then reluctantly approached an interpreter. Pointing to the line that said, "Check one: ____ Male ____ Female," she signed to the interpreter, "Me—which one?"

One of Emily's fears in going to this agency was realized. She was forced to display what she thought of as her "ignorance" and lack of education. She was not confused about her gender, but "girl" or "woman" were the only words she knew that described it.

Deafness is an invisible disability that only becomes apparent when the deaf person attempts to communciate. Deafness that occurs at birth or in the first years of life has a profound impact on the acquisition of language. Language acquisition occurs later than it does for children who can hear. Moreover, the majority of deaf children learn to communicate in American Sign Language, which differs grammatically and syntactically from English (Stokoe, 1960). This latter factor further impedes communication between the deaf and hearing worlds. Thus, deafness interferes with communication, in particular, with information and points of view of the hearing world that are conveyed in conversation and in the media, a major agent of social change. The linguistic/communicative gap that separates deaf people from the rest of society creates a cultural lag that is nowhere more apparent than in the place of deaf women in our society.

Deafness encompasses a range of social, emotional, and cultural experiences that are unique to persons who are deaf (Rainer et al., 1963). A profound hearing impairment early in life interferes with the socialization process. In all societies parents socialize their children by communicating cultural norms through language. Parents' behavior towards others is also an important factor in socializing children, since children overhear what their elders say to each other and combine these with their observations of adult behavior to develop norms for social behavior.

Deafness that occurs early in life interferes with the linguistic means of transmitting culture, and without language, the nuances of the socialization process are lost on deaf children. The great majority of deaf persons have hearing parents with whom they cannot communicate and whose value system differs in subtle but significant ways from their own. One hearing mother said of her adult deaf child, "You know, some of Betty's ideas come from that school she went to. They taught her to think different than if she had been brought up in the family. They took her [mind] away from me." Delayed language and socialization have tremendous significance for the problems deaf persons face in adulthood.

Eight percent of deaf people have deaf parents (Schein and Delk, 1974) and thus have a viable means of communicating with and learning from their parents through sign language. This small percentage of deaf people develop language skills at the same time that other developmental skills take place. At an early age they experiment with the language, as do children who can hear. They are a part of their parents' world, and they imitate, observe, and comprehend what is going on around them. In adulthood, deaf persons who have deaf parents usually have a well-developed ability to express and understand both their native language, American Sign Language, and signed English. Meadow (1968) found that such children have a higher sense of self-esteem than children whose parents could hear. They were socialized primarily by their own parents and have a strong identification with deafness that carries them through life.

In contrast, most deaf persons did not begin to acquire language until they went to school at the age of five or six years. Entry into school was an emotional experience whether children were sent to state residential schools or to day schools. Suddenly, the child was put into the company of others with the same problem, and they began to learn the language together. Language acquisition and socialization thus took place concurrently for the majority of deaf children.

Most deaf persons have stayed in school until they were 18 years old, spending 12 years in the institution. The recent pattern has been for children to board at school during the week and go home for the weekends, regardless of the proximity of their family homes. In the past, older persons usually spent the entire year at the institution, going home only in the summer. The separation of the child from the family has weakened the parent-child bond in many instances, a factor that places limits on deaf women's resources in adulthood.

Until recently, institutions for deaf children were highly segregated by gender and, as a result, girls spent considerable time together with female teachers and counselors who instilled traditional American values about the role of deaf women in society.

When deaf children were at home with their families, the inability to communicate with parents created strained relationships. The frequent complaint, by deaf women and men alike, that they were left out of conversation at the dinner table, symbolizes the status of the deaf person in the family as "second class citizen."

During these formative years, the peer group was formed and the child learned to rely heavily on other children for emotional support and information about the world. This pattern is maintained in adulthood. The social and emotional reliance on one's peers and the strong identification with other deaf persons that takes place in childhood combine to perpetuate the deaf community.

American Sign Language

American Sign Language (ASL) is a visual language that is not based on English. As previously noted, it has its own syntactical and grammatical structure (Stokoe, 1960). For example, the question, "Have you finished eating?'' would be signed "Finish eat?'' in ASL with the accompaniment of appropriate body language. Few deaf people have language competency in both ASL and spoken English.

ASL has its own set of at least 45 different handshapes—parallel to English's 26 alphabet letters. ASL also has a great variety of hand movements: slow, quick, long, short, repetitive. ASL is a standard sign language in the United States, but it has its own visual dialects depending on the part of the country in which it is being used. ASL users can readily tell where deaf people have come from or what schools they have attended in the past. ASL has its own inflections, all in facial expressions. Words for which there are no sign equivalents or for which signs are not known can be fingerspelled, using the manual alphabet. ASL is used by about 85 percent of the deaf population (for a good discussion of ASL, see Wilbur, 1979).

ASL has been called "the language of the outhouse" (Meadow, 1972), since for many years sign language was forbidden, especially in classrooms. Children were forced to use the oral method to communicate with others. Children who used their hands to communicate were often punished by having their hands slapped (Higgins, 1980). Sign language continued to be used, but in secret. The stigmatizing circumstances under which many deaf persons learned and began using sign language has had its impact on the language and on the level of linguistic sophistication of many sign language users. The signs themselves often tell a story about the frustrations of ineffective education. For example, one composite sign stands for "Too many big words." There are signs that indicate negative self-image, such as "dummy" and "pea-brain," and deaf people often apologize to hearing persons or to more highly educated deaf persons with comments such as "Me dummy—know nothing."

These negative feelings about self and about the language are countered by the tremendous symbolic significance of the language. ASL is the symbolic badge of identity in the deaf community. Since many persons were "starved" for a means of communication in childhood before they learned sign language, there is immense pride in the language. Its resilience is a testimony to deaf perseverance. In groups of deaf people, sign language becomes bigger and bolder than in public. Facial expression and body language take on new dimensions, and the richness of the language is exploited to its fullest. Such social events are the high points around which deaf social life pivots, and provide the nurturance needed to deal with the problems of everyday life.

Life in the Deaf Community

Deaf persons tend to congregate in urban areas where the potential for finding a job and for meeting other deaf people is greatest. The hub of the deaf community is the "deaf club," a term used by deaf persons themselves to describe one type of deaf organization that is scattered throughout most U.S. cities. The deaf club and its meaning for deaf people is central to social life and a play entitled "Tales from a Deaf Club," has been written by two deaf playwrights. (For an excellent description of the deaf community, see Higgins, 1980.)

The persons that emerged as leaders in the deaf community either had lost their hearing after they acquired language or, as noted earlier, had deaf parents themselves. This small minority tended to excel academically, and frequently went to college and entered professional careers while carrying out leadership roles in the deaf community. The acknowledged leaders were almost always men. Although there have been almost as many educated, professional women in the deaf community as men, female leaders have begun to receive acknowledgement of their leadership abilities only in the last few years. Nevertheless, change is slow to occur. For example, a recent women's meeting during a national convention attended by one of the authors was conducted by a man. The appropriateness of male leadership at a women's meeting was not questioned by the audience.

In contrast to the select few who became professionals, most prelingually deaf children had difficulty learning English and other academic subjects. They were prepared for sex-stereotyped careers. Boys were taught carpentry and printing, while girls were prepared to become seamstresses, homemakers, or keypunch operators. The focus on traditional activities began a pattern maintained at home by hearing parents because it required a minimum of communication. Inability to communicate between hearing parent and deaf child was thus a factor in reinforcing sex role stereotypes.

Parents of deaf daughters frequently neglect to prepare their daughter for coping with everyday life in adulthood. Becker (1980) found that the period of early adulthood was highly stressful because of this lack of preparation. Informants repeatedly said that they were ignorant of the ways of the world, that no one had explained what life outside the institution would be like. One exception to this pattern was a woman who stated that her mother had taught her everything she knew. Her mother even took her with her when she was planning her husband's funeral "because someday this will happen to you." She contrasted her own experience favorably with those of her friends, who were "lost" when they were first forced to handle such matters.

Parents hoped that their daughters would eventually marry and that their husbands would take care of them. In fact, the majority of deaf women marry deaf men (Jacobs, 1974), who often have been as poorly prepared for the roles and responsibilities of adulthood as their wives have been. As a result, deaf women frequently become the family managers, balancing their roles as wives, mothers, and full-time workers while doing much of the family decision-making.

Deaf Families

Sandra Jackson sat on the faded couch in the sparsely furnished living room of her rented suburban house, and talked about her life. From the Midwest, she was born deaf and was sent to the state school for the deaf when she was five years old. After that, she only saw her family when she went home to the family farm for Christmas and summer vacations. They could not communicate with her. When she left school at 18, she stayed in the city where she had gone to school and got a job in a factory. When some of her deaf friends decided to move to California, she came with them. Six months after she arrived, she met her husband, a printer, at a deaf club social. Shortly after they married she became pregnant and left the work force.

Sandra is now 37 years old and has four children between the ages of 8 and 15. The oldest child, a girl, has been raised to be the family interpreter, since interpreting is viewed as an appropriate female role. She often interprets between her parents and the younger children who have never become proficient in sign language.

Three years ago Sandra went back to work over her husband's objections. "[It was] boring sitting at home all day—cut off from the world. I felt very isolated."[1] Sandra has had two jobs since whe went back to work, first as a figure clerk in an insurance company, and more recently as an aide in an agency serving deaf people. Her current job has led her to reflect on the difficulties she experienced when she was a housewife. "I was ignorant of my rights. I thought of my inability to communicate with hearing people as my problem, not theirs. I didn't know what was going on in the world around me. There was nowhere to turn when I had a problem."

She is especially bitter about the impact of the communication barrier on her and her children. "I never had an interpreter when I went to the hospital for my children's births. The first time I was really scared . . . I didn't know what was happening. No one told me what to expect. Later on, when the kids were getting older, I struggled with writing notes back and forth to the kids' doctors and school counselors. It was a waste of time. I never understood what people were trying to tell me. . . . When a child was sick, I never knew just how serious it was, or what I could do if one of them was having trouble in school. I get angry just thinking about it."

About work she says, "When I first went back to work, I would take the lowest pay—just grateful for a job. My husband kept saying, 'A woman's place is in the home,' but I was glad to get out and make $3 an hour—and most deaf women are satisfied with that.''

Sandra's husband still does not approve of her working, although the extra income is needed. In addition to her paycheck, she brings home too many new ideas. He complained in private, ''She is always demanding an interpreter now when she has to go to school about the kids. She kept asking for a raise until she got one—and then she talked about it with her friends. It makes me look bad with the deaf—as if I can't take care of my family. Last week she even complained to a friend that I never babysat the kids when they were little.''

Sandra has not had contact with her own family since she left the Midwest almost 20 years ago. She relies on five or six deaf women friends for mutual support and companionship. She sees them often and shares with them the information she has access to in her new job. She is beginning to take on leadership activities in the deaf community, and sees herself as an advocate for deaf women and their needs. She is patient about her husband's attitude most of the time. She says, ''It's hard on him being deaf. He's very cautious. He thinks deaf people are at the mercy of the hearing world, and that we have to be more careful than they (hearing people) do. He's afraid if we ask for anything, we will lose what we've got.''

Like hearing women, the majority of deaf women eventually marry (71.5 percent of deaf women marry by age 34, Schein and Delk, 1974). There is an increasing tendency for young deaf people to live together without getting legally married. While this practice reflects an increasing tendency in our society in general, it is also an outcome of the laws surrounding the Supplemental Social Security Income System (SSI). Many young deaf people who are untrained and unemployed qualify for SSI. If two persons who receive SSI marry, however, the amount they receive is reduced. Consequently, many young deaf people in their twenties and thirties remain legally unmarried so that they can continue to receive maximum benefits from SSI. The effect of this trend on family organization in the deaf community is as yet unknown.

It is the cultural norm for deaf women to play a passive role and for deaf men to play a dominant role in the marital relationship, a model that is perpetuated by institutional socialization. These roles may be reversed in private, but in public individuals try to demonstrate culturally appropriate behavior that will maintain the status quo. This is one of many ways in which deaf persons try to normalize their behavior to their conception of ''normative'' American social behavior. Conformity to such a norm serves important functions, especially for those who must continually deal with their own nonconformity.

The majority of deaf couples have children who can hear. Only 9.1 percent of deaf couples have deaf children (Schein and Delk, 1974). Hearing children are used as interpreters, and parents also rely on them to explain customs, news, and other information gleaned from the hearing world. The oldest hearing daughter is usually given this responsibility, and sometimes even becomes an interpreter between the parents and younger children.

The manner in which deaf parents were socialized in school settings inevitably affects how they socialize their own children. Many deaf couples use rules of discipline from their own school experience for raising their children. Since these rules were established for handling large numbers of children, they are often overly rigid. Problems between parents and children may develop as a result.

A number of women find careers as teachers and counselors in schools for the deaf, and frequently remain single. Although marriage is highly valued in the deaf community, a single person who works in an institutional setting becomes a part of the on-going social activities connected with the school. Since a continual round of social events is characteristic of these schools, the school becomes a substitute for one's own family. Single workers in the institution are not isolated from their peers as single deaf persons who work outside the system often are.

Women who deviate from these patterns in the deaf community are not easily accepted. Lesbians are frequently ostracized and often remain on the fringe of the community.

Needs of Deaf Women

As deaf women grow up, leave school, and begin to take on the roles of adult life, communication barriers continue to intervene in their adaptation. Despite the multiple roles that deaf women have traditionally carried out, they often manage without the emotional and social supports available to other women. Deaf women struggle to develop and maintain family cohesiveness without adequate preparation for marriage and motherhood, and their responsibilities in these roles. Nor are they prepared for the crises of family life, such as separation, divorce, or illness.

Information about birth control, marital rights, child-rearing techniques and other practical aspects of marriage and family life is frequently lacking. Thus, lack of access to information that is disseminated to the public through the media severely restricts deaf women's options. Deaf women are not privy to information that has become commonplace to many American women because of the linguistic and communication differences that exist. These, in turn, affect deaf women's level of sophistication on various subjects. For example, the changing status of the birth control pill as a health risk is a subject that assumes considerable knowledge of health and health practices. The majority of deaf women have little information on such a topic. Instead, when a deaf woman wants information about a medication, she relies on her peer group. She may approach a person she considers knowledgeable, hold out the medication, and ask, "Is this all right for me to take?"

Although there are no direct data on the subject, it is likely that because of the limited communication experienced between deaf women and their hearing families deaf women rely significantly less than hearing women do on their mothers and other relatives for information, help, and emotional support. The lack of role models and familial supports forces deaf women to turn to each other to meet their needs.

Early in life the deaf individual begins to develop a broad base of friendship in school. This peer group forms the basis for social support that helps to sustain the individual amidst the ongoing difficulties of everyday life (Becker, 1980). Bonds between women are particularly helpful in coping with everyday problems of living, as they give each other advice and share experiences.

Identification with the deaf community, begun in childhood, becomes an important part of the coping mechanisms that deaf women develop. This identification is reinforced by negative experiences in the hearing world that underline the difficulties of communication. As a result, deaf women have extremely restricted resources, usually limited to their peers and to the few agencies that serve the deaf community in any locale.

Lack of access to the media and other informational networks, poor English language skills, and distrust of the hearing world result in the use of social activities as opportunities to obtain and pass on information. Since the communication barrier is a deterrent to information retrieval, the information that does get through is often incorrect and is subject to further modification as it is passed from one person to the next. This situation is accentuated among deaf women who are members of ethnic minorities. They experience even greater problems in communication than other deaf women, and are particularly hesitant to seek out available resources. For example, one black woman came to an agency used by deaf people in an advanced state of pregnancy because she had no financial resources to live on. When questioned about when she thought her baby was due, she said, "In about 10 months."

When we compare the deaf woman's access to resources with those of hearing women, it becomes apparent that the deaf woman is separated from services by the communication barrier imposed by the disability. This barrier places great limitations on the deaf woman by preventing her from obtaining knowledge that would help her to cope with the events of daily life as well as with life crises. There are two types of knowledge to which she has little access: (1) social knowledge, usually gleaned through informal conversations and overhearing other people talk; (2) formal knowledge from various media such as television, books, and magazines.

The lack of information has a dramatic effect on the quality of daily life for deaf people. What is more, change occurs slowly, often considerably behind the rest of society. The following example illustrates the extent of this informational vacuum. An 18-year-old woman showed up at an agency that serves deaf persons and confided to a staff member that she thought she was pregnant. In the course of the interview that followed, she was asked if she had ever used birth control of any kind. Her response was, "What's that?"

Recommendations for the Provision of Services

The needs of deaf women are related to information and to access. Ways in which deaf women's needs may be met by providers fall into three categories: (1) educational programs such as workshops for deaf women of all ages; (2) visual information presented through the media; (3) access to health and social services. In all of these areas active participation of deaf women in planning and carrying out a program is a necessity to ensure success.

Educational Programs for Deaf Women

The structure of the deaf community lends itself to information dissemination through the workshop format. Information can be tailored for presentation to a group of deaf women and at the same time allow them to discuss new ideas with each other in privacy. The kinds of subjects appropriate to such a format include (but are not limited to): women's rights, health, job skills, development of leadership skills, marital relations, and parenting. Participation of deaf women in the presentation of material is optimum and will enhance learning.

Deaf women should also be encouraged to attend workshops developed for the general public. Before this goal becomes a reality, however, the general knowledge of deaf women must approach that of their hearing contemporaries. In addition, certified sign language interpreters must be readily available. Deaf women should also be encouraged to keep up with the rapidly changing status of American women.

Visual Information Through the Media

In addition to programs that enhance and develop social and coping skills, deaf women need access to information of a didactic nature. For example, there is a growing movement in the United States to make television news programs accessible to deaf viewers through signs or captions. This effort has done much to keep deaf persons current with the state of the world around them.

Television and other visual media could also be used to provide education and to enlarge the linguistic abilities of deaf women. Programs designed specifically for deaf women could do much to increase the scope of information a deaf woman has at her disposal, for example, information about career options.

As an educational medium, television is probably the most effective tool in providing on-going education to deaf women. In contrast to the negative experiences many women had with formal education in school, television has the potential to develop ways of transmitting information to deaf women in new and exciting ways.

Access to Health and Social Services

Concurrent with an increase in the level of information available to deaf women is the need for services. As mentioned earlier, negative experiences in seeking services in the past have led deaf women to avoid "hearing" agencies. Providers who wish to make their services available to deaf women need to work with women in their local deaf community in planning, advertising, and delivering services. Service delivery systems must make a concerted effort to inform deaf women about the services they offer. The importance of utilizing the informal grapevine of the deaf community to advertise programs cannot be too highly stressed, nor can the appearance of providers at deaf social events to advertise and informally discuss their programs. Staff members who are deaf and certified interpreters who are available at regular times ensure optimum participation of deaf consumers (Becker and Nadler, 1980). Education aimed at staff members of facilities that intend to provide services and education is equally important so that staff will understand deaf culture and the special needs and concerns of deaf women.

Services to deaf women, particularly in specialized areas such as family planning services, should be undertaken by agencies serving the general public after conducting a needs assessment in the local deaf community. It is not possible nor is it desirable for agencies serving the deaf community exclusively to attempt to meet all the needs of deaf women. Indeed, the specialization of services inherent in complex, urban society presents a bewildering array to the deaf woman in search of solutions to problems she shares with all other women. Service delivery systems thus need to become aware of the deaf woman and her needs as a consumer and be able to respond appropriately to referrals, whether or not they routinely offer services to deaf women.

To summarize, the success of any new program for deaf women depends on inclusion of the following points:

1. The new program should be extensively advertised in the deaf community, using word-of-mouth, printed material, and personal appearances by providers and key deaf consumers at social events.
2. Certified sign language interpreters should be used wherever appropriate. A rudimentary knowledge of sign language, e.g., knowing the signs for a few key words, helps to bridge the communication barrier, but the provider should not hesitate to use an interpreter after demonstrating an interest in sign language, so that communication will be clear. Certified sign language interpreters should be available at regular times, e.g., 9:00-12:00 Monday mornings, so that clients can plan accordingly.
3. Wherever possible, deaf personnel should be employed to work with other staff in providing services to deaf clients. Employment of deaf persons facilitates the acceptance of the program by deaf persons, enhances the education of staff, and normalizes the presence of deaf persons in the service delivery system.
4. The hearing staff should be educated about the culture of deafness and ways of communicating, utilizing deaf persons to provide the bulk of the information.

Conclusion

Deaf women in the deaf community are considered "second class citizens," based on the tendency of all deaf persons to imitate the values of the larger society. The conservatism of the deaf community in attempting to conform to cultural norms accentuates the culture lag that is related to the communication barrier.

Awareness of one's options and the ability to control one's life decreases the sense of frustration and powerlessness so frequently expressed by deaf women. As equal access to information and services takes place, the deaf woman's isolation will decrease and she will become more involved as a member of society. This involvement will not only affect her but her family, her friends, and her community as well. She will be better able to utilize the strengths of the deaf community when she has access to services. Ultimately, increased access will result in greater self-determination for all deaf women.

Note

1. All quotes have been translated into English.

References

Becker, G. 1983. *Growing Old in Silence*. Berkeley: University of California Press.
————, and G. Nadler. 1980. "The aged deaf: Integration of a disabled group into an agency serving elderly people." *Gerontologist* 20: 214-21.

Higgins, P. 1980. *Outsiders in a Hearing World*. Beverly Hills: Sage Publications.

Jacobs, L. 1974. *A Deaf Man Speaks Out*. Washington, D.C.: Gallaudet College Press.

Meadow, K. P. 1968. "Parental response to the medical ambiguities of deafness." *Journal of Health and Social Behavior* 9: 299-309.

———. 1972. "Sociolinguistics, sign language, and the deaf subculture." In T. O' Rourke (ed.), *Psycholinguistics and Total Communication: The State of the Art*. Washington D.C.: American Annals of the Deaf. Pp. 19-33.

Rainer, J. D., K. Altschuler, and F. J. Kallman. 1963. *Family and Mental Health Problems in a Deaf Population*. New York: Columbia University Press.

Schein, J. and M. T. Delk. 1974. *The Deaf Population in the United States*. Silver Spring, Md.: National Association of the Deaf.

Stokoe, W. C. 1960. *Sign Language Structure: An Outline of the Visual Communication Systems of the American Deaf*. Buffalo, N.Y.: Occasional Papers, No. 8, University of Buffalo.

Wilbur, R. B. 1979. *American Sign Language and Sign Systems*. Baltimore: University Park Press.

4

Multiple Minority Groups: A Case Study of Physically Disabled Women

Mary Jo Deegan

In general, disenfranchised Americans are becoming increasingly aware of their social restrictions and limited opportunities. There are now minority groups who have identified their shared problems only within the last 20 years, and these groups are rapidly changing the nature of minority relations. In particular, people with newly defined multiple minority statuses are beginning to articulate their specialized interests and establish new relations with both the dominant majority and the separate minority groups to which they belong. Physically disabled women are one such group. As women and as disabled people, they are members of two separate minority groups. Their relations to disabled males and able-bodied females shed light on the theoretical complexities of this recent social phenomenon. Understanding the specific problems of disabled women can advance theoretical and practical efforts to build a more liberated and liberating society.

Introduction[1]

More and more individuals in modern society are aware of others like themselves who are the victims of limited opportunities, hostility, or trivialization:

> At no time since the Civil War has American society been so conscious of the problems of minority groups. Not only has social action acquired a new impetus in the implementation of rights for the traditionally recognized minority groups, but ever widening social categories are being posed as candidates for minority group status (Hacker, 1971: 65).

For example, individuals who are fat, female,[2] physically disabled, gay, or labelled mentally ill now define themselves as members of minority groups while 10 to 20 years ago they may not have done so.[3] As a consequence, they are organizing for greater recognition of their problems and their right to define who they are and what they can do. Moreover, the number of people who recognize that they are prejudicially treated is rapidly increasing. Three trends are occurring at once: (1) a new subjective awareness of objective discrimination, (2) a broadening of definitions of categories eligible for minority group identification, and (3) a dramatic increase in the number of people included within these new groups.

Each of these trends has generated a new group phenomenon: the multiple minority group. This chapter is addressed specifically to defining the latter group and analyzing their effect on majority and minority relations. This is done first by examining the theoretical concepts of "minority status," "minority group," "the single minority group," "multiple minority statuses," "multiple minority group," and the "interaction effects of the multiple minority group." These concepts are then extended to an analysis of one specific multiple minority group: physically disabled women. For this case study, physically disabled women must be seen as separate from, but related to, their "single minority groups" of women and the physically disabled. After defining these relationships theoretically, a brief review of the literature concerning physically disabled women is presented and the relationships of disabled women to the single minority groups are examined.

From this completed analysis, the conclusion summarizes why this multiple minority group concept is central to our understanding of minority rights. This concept clarifies the number of people who are oppressed in this society, the process of continuing such massive discrimination, and the participation in this process of disenfranchisement by all members of this society. Therefore, we link theory and practice as interconnected units for action.

The Multiple Minority Group: Definition of Concepts

A *minority group* is any group of people who, because of their physical or cultural characteristics, are singled out from the others in the society in which they live for differential and unequal treatment, and who therefore regard themselves as objects of collective discrimination (Wirth, 1945: 347, emphasis added).

Using Wirth's definition of a minority group, it is clear that there are two conditions that must be met: an objective condition of differential or unequal treatment (a "minority status") and a subjective awareness of this group basis for discrimination. (Frequently, minority statuses exist for years without the emergence of a minority group.)

A minority group with one subjective group identification is defined here as a "single minority group." However, members of a single minority group can have a number of minority statuses, called here "multiple minority statuses." This latter term refers to the objective condition of differential and unequal treatment that arises from being singled out by others in a society as being a member of more than one minority group. The individuals or groups being singled out for this type of discriminatory treatment need not be aware of the multiple origin of the prejudicial responses.

A "multiple minority group," then, is any group of people who are singled out from the others in the society in which they live for differential and unequal treatment because they are defined as members of more than one minority group, and who therefore regard themselves as objects of this combination of collective discriminations.

The emergent patterns of inequality are not identical to those imposed on any single minority group. Instead, there are "interaction effects of the multiple minority group." These are the unique patterns of differential and unequal treatment based upon the combined characteristics of the multiple minority group. These interaction effects generate two processes particular to the multiple minority group: (1) the differential and unequal treatment is usually more severely limiting for the multiple minority group compared to a single minority group, and (2) the groups of people discriminating against the multiple minority group may include members of both the "majority" and "single minority groups." Multiple minority groups alter the relationships between the majority and "minorities" by generating new patterns of discrimination within minority groups.

Before proceeding to an analysis of a specific multiple minority group—physically disabled women—the concept defined here will be examined in greater detail.

Discussing the Concepts

As noted above, a person may have multiple minority statuses, and the number of devalued statuses could range from two to several. There is, in fact, a tendency for one minority status to precipitate entry into another. For example, a major indicator of a minority status is a limitation on rights to free entry and mobility in the marketplace (Reich, Gordon, and Edwards, 1973, for a discussion of "labor market segmentation"). Economic restrictions, however, are not a necessary condition for defining a minority group. Blacks and women, for example, may be members of the middle or upper classes and yet still be subject to prejudicial treatment in their everyday lives.

Nonetheless, membership in a minority group is likely to generate other minority statuses, including lower statuses related to restrictions in economic resources. For instance, women who are elderly tend to have a limited and low income. They are likely to be widows and to develop physical disabilities and perhaps become so overwhelmed by their everyday limitations that they become depressed (Markson and Hess, 1980). The multiple problem family has long been noted in the literature on social welfare, but the identification of multiple minority groups with unique multiple problems has not been emphasized.

Although the multiple minority identification is becoming more frequent, this does not mean that the individual with multiple minority statuses becomes a part of a multiple minority group. Instead, multiple minority groups tend to share only two or perhaps three minority statuses. This is due to a variety of reasons:

1. There may be an awareness of only one minority group status. As noted in Wirth's definition of a "minority group," there must be an awareness of collective discrimination. A person with multiple minority statuses may recognize only one of them as limiting; for example, there are a number of writings on black women or Chicanas as oppressed primarily as a function of their race or ethnicity, respectively, but not by their status as females (see discussions in Stone, 1975, and Cotera, 1980).
2. The number of people who share more than one minority status is smaller than the number who comprise the minority groups in which they are members. For example, there are fewer black women than black men and women; or there are fewer disabled women in poverty than there are disabled people. As each additional minority status is added, there are fewer members within the subgroups.
3. As the number of multiple minority statuses increases, the likelihood of decreased social and economic resources also increases (e.g., limited entry into the professions, low-income employment, and minimal educational opportunities). For example, lesbians have a smaller group of accepting and powerful peers who share their status than do heterosexual white women.
4. There is a limitation on how much time can be spent working within groups organizing for social change. Activists for a minority cause usually need to find time to work on these projects while having obligations at home or in the marketplace which restrict their "extra" resources for political organizing and community action.
5. Finally, there is an interaction effect. Multiple minorities are the most disenfranchised members of society. It is more difficult to define and defend a "new" minority than to work with an established, legitimated minority group. The multiple minority group can most easily battle for their rights in more powerful groups, particularly powerful minority groups in which they share membership. Because of each of the above factors, multiple minority groups rarely share more than three minority statuses.

It is important to note again the relative recentness of group awareness for many minorities.[4] This subjective dimension appears to be an emergent process derived from the increasing awareness of blacks during the 1950's of their limited civil rights and their subsequent battles as a minority group to eliminate these oppressions. This civil rights work, in turn, led to the recognition by other groups of their own minority statuses. During the 1960's, women became more articulate in their demands for social recognition, and then the Gay Rights movement became more outspoken in reference to their restricted life options (lesbians particularly organized out of their contacts with women's groups). During the 1970's, these trends for more and more recognition of minority groups became ground swells in reference to a number of "new" minority groups; particularly the institutionalized. Whether children, mentally ill, mentally retarded, physically disabled, imprisoned, or elderly, these new minority groups began to demand more of their caretakers and of the community.

As each of these groups became more articulate and demanded more from the social system and society, it became apparent that there were multiple minority statuses with conflicting demands for recognition of their problem as "the most important." Thus, inter-minority conflicts emerged: for example, "straight versus lesbian" feminists and "white versus black" feminists. Within the black, Chicano/a and American Indian Movements, some members protested that their leaders were too "white-identified" or too removed from the problems of the "poorer," or "less educated" minority member. Many of these conflicts were seen both within and outside of these groups as problems within the minority groups and sometimes as indicators of their unstable membership or lack of organization. But other analyses are possible. Here, these are interpreted as signs of minority versus multiple minority relations. For example, a multiple minority group with two minority statuses may be discriminated against by two major groups: the dominant majority and the single identified minority group. For illustration, poor blacks may be discriminated against or even economically exploited by wealthy blacks as well as by whites. In this case, class interests may divide a group that is victimized by an even more powerful group.[5]

The concept of a "multiple minority group" aids in interpreting minority relations. The concept breaks down the rigidity of many minority analyses which consider the minority as one group and the majority as another. Unfortunately, this latter thinking generates strong hostility and barriers between an "in-group" and an "out-group." Taking the "male" versus "female" argument as an illustration, it is unequivocally true that men receive far more structural benefits from this society than do women. It first appears that approximately 51 percent of the population (female) is oppressed by the other 49 percent (male). But the percentage of oppressed is quickly altered by including minority men, whether black, American Indian, Puerto Rican, Chicano, or Asian American, as also victimized in this society. Some white men are also limited in their rights to full participation: notably Appalachians, Jews, the physically handicapped, homosexuals, the mentally ill, the incarcerated, and to some degree, the fat male.[6] In addition, there are some specific, localized prejudices that are oppressive for white men who are members of other ethnic group or religious minorities.

Instead of a simplistic "us" versus "them" argument, as the number of minority groups increases, the relations within and between groups become increasingly complex. Simultaneously, as the number of people in multiple minority groups increases, even more complex interaction effects emerge. Perhaps an affluent black man has significantly less unequal treatment than an impoverished white woman. Perhaps a poor white woman receives significantly less unequal treatment relative to a gay, white male from Appalachia. Clearly, an answer to the question of interaction effects cannot be given without extensive, empirical analysis. But even at this early stage of analysis, it is possible to see that American society tends to operate within a "dog-eat-dog" minority relations cycle. Instead of the overall rising of each minority with the entry of a new minority group into society—which was seen in the past with waves of immigration in the United States (Park, 1926)—perhaps we are beginning to experience a multiple, layered effect where portions of a minority group rise while other segments remain at the same level or sink relative to other minority groups. A recent example of this is the rising status of black males. Economically, black and white females show greater similarity in income than do black females and males (Almquist and Wehrle-Einhorn, 1978). Minority groups are becoming more complex and developing new relations to a numerically smaller "majority." Simultaneously, they confront new tensions within their own minority groups. These new strains, moreover, may generate a minority within another minority group—a multiple minority group—so that the "outsider" becomes the "dominant" minority group as well as "the majority".

In addition to these multiple minority identifications, there is a potential for more integration in our society. As the members of one minority group begin to perceive the similarities of their status with another minority group, the definitions of "in-group" and "out-group" change. For example, if blacks and women perceived their similar, disadvantaged statuses they could form a larger number of united Americans (these similarities are outlined in Hacker, 1951).

Despite this positive potential for coalition politics, the strongest identifications tend to remain with one's own minority group. This is particularly true for the multiple minority groups who have a larger number of powerful groups restricting their freedoms. In addition, the multiple minority group does have problems separate from other groups. Although alliances can be made, the special interests of the multiple minority need to be articulated, defended, and addressed. Finally, the multiple minority group may have more serious problems than the single minority group, or it may develop new strengths as a result of its unique situation.

Although in general it is expected that the multiple minority also has multiple problems, there may also be the phenomenon of the "freedom" or "strength" of multiple problems which allow the individual to totally disregard the standards and evaluations of the majority because there is no hope of ever becoming a part of it. This phenomenon is not to be confused with the prejudicial "they (e.g., poor, fat, blacks) are happier" generalization. Instead this is a phenomenon based on the ability to break through the prejudicial limitations of others because they are revealed as too bizarre, too impossible of realization, or too discriminatory to be taken seriously. Clearly, this is a difficult individual recognition, but collectively it may emerge as a characteristic of a group under the same structural strains. Epstein, for example, finds that black women professionals are both so discriminated against and so strong, that because of their high "majority" achievement in education and occupations, they become particularly competent and successful (1973). Although this particular study has been questioned (Stone, 1979), it does illustrate the possibility of interaction effects with multiple minority groups that are generally unexamined at this time.[7] This lack of information is particularly true for physically disabled women, who are examined in more detail below.

Physically Disabled Women

The separate literatures on women and the physically disabled as disadvantaged groups in this society are extensive. (for the former, see de Beauvoir, 1970; Huber, 1973; Freeman, 1979; Daly, 1978 and for the latter see Safilios-Rothschild, 1970; Albrecht, 1975; Wright, 1960; Barker, et al., 1955). No attempt is made to summarize all of these writings here. Instead, the multiple minority status of physically disabled women is the focus.

This multiple minority group is an emergent of the recent surge of interest in the women's movement, starting in the 1960's, and the physically disabled movement, starting in the mid-1970's. One indication of both the neglect of physically disabled women and their particularly oppressed status is found in the minuscule amount of information available on them. For example, a computer search of *Psychological Abstracts* revealed over 7,500 entries on disabled and over 3,300 entries on women, but only 31 articles on disabled women. Within this small set, 19 concerned women with cancer, predominantly breast cancer. The research conducted on disabled women is very limited and analysis of their experience in the marketplace is particularly hard to find.

With an estimated 36 million disabled people in the United States (O'Toole and Weeks, 1978: 1), there are probably 18 million disabled women. The figure may actually be significantly higher due to two facts: (1) there are more elderly disabled women than elderly disabled men, because women have greater longevity than men and the elderly have a higher proportion of disabilities relative to other age groups, and (2) there are slightly more women than men in the general population. Even without adjusting the figure of 18 million disabled women, there are millions of disabled women subjected to discrimination in a variety of ways. It is sobering and upsetting to realize that so little information is available concerning this multiple minority group.

Physically Disabled and Able-Bodied Women: Their Common and Separate Interests

Both of these groups suffer from discrimination in the marketplace, in self-limiting attitudes learned through sex role socialization, in a lack of appreciation of the strength and nature of female sexuality, and access to and control over information concerning reproduction. In each of these areas, however, physically disabled women have more restrictions than able-bodied women. This greater restrictiveness can be illustrated by comparing the market performance of the two groups.

In 1980, the average woman worker earned $11,500, while the average man earned $19,712. Among full-time workers, women's wages were approximately 60% of that earned by men (U.S. Department of Commerce, 1981). Moreover, women's work is largely conducted in sex-segregated occupations and in "pink-collar" ghettos (Howe, 1977). As dismal as this picture is, that of disabled women is strikingly worse:

> The vast majority of disabled women in the United States are unskilled after 12 years of public education, able to identify few career options, and society as a whole remains unaware of their existence (O'Toole and Weeks, 1978: 22).

Thus, the interest of able-bodied and disabled women can be defined as very similar, with the added proviso that disabled women are often discriminated against even more severely than their able-bodied sisters. Given this perspective of shared restrictions, both women's groups can gain from joining forces. Nonetheless, there are at least three major barriers to joint identification: (1) discrimination against feminists by disabled women, (2) discrimination against the disabled by able-bodied women, and (3) their counter-definitions of problems.

The first two types of prejudice are products of sexism and able-bodism, and they can be understood in a straight-forward fashion.[8] It should be noted that able-bodism is *structurally* more oppressive to disabled women than sexism by disabled women is oppressive to able-bodied women. Able-bodied people have access to a far greater number of needed resources than the disabled. The able-bodied more frequently restrict access to those resources needed by the disabled than the disabled restrict access to resources needed by able-bodied women.

The third barrier (conflicting definitions of problems confronting the two groups) is a more subtle and difficult barrier to positive inter-group identifications than those barriers generated by the two types of prejudice noted above. Therefore, this third problem is discussed in greater depth here.

One of the few published papers addressing the issue of disabled women and feminism was written by Deborah Kent in 1977. In this article, she articulates the problems of conflicting interests between a minority group and its multiple minority group members. As a member of a woman's consciousness-raising group, she found that as a disabled woman she was indignant at the others' description and analysis of their problems:

> But it was impossible for me to confess my own reaction to their tales of horror, which was a very real sense of envy. Society had provided a place for them as women, however restricting that place might be, and they knew it. For myself and for other disabled women, sex discrimination is a secondary issue—in life and in the job market (Kent, 1977: 18).

Kent's argument is a clear statement of a common mistrust of able-bodied women and feminists by disabled women. The latter's description of able-bodied women's situations goes something like this: "These women's lives are good so why don't they realize it? If they want to change things, why don't they just do it and stop complaining about minor problems?" Thus, the common core of discrimination experienced by both groups is neither expressed nor understood.

What Kent was responding to in her consciousness-raising group is her treatment as an *asexual object*, while the other women were discussing the problems of being treated as a *sexual object*. These problems in sexuality are devastating to one's personality and social status. Each problem can have vastly different results. For example, a philandering and insensitive husband can destroy a woman's self-esteem. Being considered sexually uninteresting and undesirable is equally painful, but this identification can result in the nontraditional status of never marrying.

Both women's groups have the shared experience of being objectified. Their alienation from the self and the sense of powerlessness over sexual expression and appreciation are both manifestations of this commonality. Although there are striking divergances between the two types of objectification, both result in sexual alienation. Both are inhumane responses that are generated by more powerful males in intimate relations. Able-bodied heterosexual women frequently have the experience of believing that they are sexually "alive" and "respected." If they discover, for a variety of reasons, that this is untrue, then their sense of betrayal and frustration is quite deep. This distressing experience may be quite similar to that of a disabled women who also is not respected or valued as a sexual person because of the prejudicial perception that the disability makes her unattractive. Although the origin of these types of sexual objectification is different, the process of being evaluated as a sexual commodity is similar. There is some truth to the old adage, "'Tis better to have loved and lost than never to have loved at all", but this is not a viable solution to a group problem of sexual alienation and objectification.

This kind of misunderstanding between able-bodied and disabled women is only one example of the kind of minority group conflicts that can occur. Both groups are subject to the discriminatory myths and images of more dominant males. These stereotypes must be discussed by both groups of women before any intergroup analysis can be undertaken.

Physically disabled women, may, in fact, have more in common with disabled men who are concerned with discrimination against the handicapped and their specialized problems in barrier-free environments and the limitations of the services and industries designed to serve their special interests. Simultaneously, sexism exhibited by disabled men is a problem to be considered.

Physically Disabled Women and Men: Their Common and Separate Interests

One of the powers of minority group recognition is the ability to articulate common experiences and struggles. In this sense, disabled men and women have a deep and common bond. Sexism within this movement, however, is a barrier to the formation of such bonds. Sexism in this context arises from three main sources: (1) the agency personnel who interact with disabled women, (2) a segment of the disabled population who lack an awareness of the reality of sexism, and (3) the structure of minority group organizations. Documentation of discrimination by service providers is the most powerful and extensive (although even this documentation is limited). This form of discrimination, therefore, is the focus of our discussion of inter-group conflicts.

Sexism by caretakers and institutions serving the disabled is extensive. This prejudice is particularly blatant in the areas of sexuality and reproductive rights. As Elle Friedman Becker, a paraplegic, notes:

> I can't help but cringe in my chair when the medical profession makes references to paraplegics' sexual "alternatives" as if by implication, we cannot enjoy normal sex (1978: xvi).

The literature on spinal cord injuries is concerned primarily with male problems of erection, orgasm, and fertility, while female sexuality is dismissed.

> The few articles that are available rarely deal with the physical aspects of sex. If they do, it is only to mention intercourse as the only means of sexual expression, and, of course, the woman is in the passive missionary position. Often they indicate a woman's sexuality is strictly related to menses, the sex act at childbirth, with no regard for women's feelings (Becker, 1978: xvi).

The sexism in this area is amply documented by Kolodny's (1972) outstanding study of long-term effects of diabetes on women's sexuality. Noting the relatively extensive documentation on impairment of sexual functioning in diabetic males, he wanted to know if there were any attendant changes in sexual response for diabetic females. To remedy this gap in knowledge, he interviewed 125 Caucasian females between the ages of 18 and 42 who had previously been diagnosed as diabetic. A control group of 100 nondiabetic women were similarly interviewed. The findings were striking:

> Forty-four of 125 diabetic women (35.2%) reported complete absence of orgasmic response during the year preceding inquiry, whereas only 6 out of 100 nondiabetic women (6.0%) reported nonorgasmic function during the same period (p. 104).

The implications of Kolodny's study are equally striking. Prior to this study, it was not even known that this link between diabetes and female orgasm existed. How many diabetic women with this disease-related impairment thought that their lack of response was a personality dysfunction, flagging interest in their partners, or poor technique? Ignorance on such a vital dimension of human sexuality could have profound effects on intimate relationships. Kolodny's study amply illustrates two important theoretical issues: that information on disabled women is scarce and that such a dearth of knowledge could have an immediate, direct impact on their everyday lives.

Although Becker and Kolodny point to discrimination in the area of sexuality, sexism also limits economic opportunities and services: disabled men receive more benefits from the rehabilitation system than women. For example, a government report published in 1976 noted that:

> 1) Disabled men were more likely to receive vocational school and/or on the job training. 2) A higher percentage of disabled men (93.1%) were rehabilitated into wage earning occupations (versus 68.5% of the disabled women). 3) The

average weekly earnings for disabled men at rehabilitation closure was significantly higher. Only 2.12% of the women, compared to 10.3% of the men, were earning $200 or more per week at closure. 4) The highest percentages of employed disabled men were located in a wider range of occupations; the highest percentages of employed disabled women clustered in fewer areas, i.e., services and clerical fields (Rehabilitation Services Administration, 1976, cited in O'Toole and Weeks, 1978).

Physically disabled women are clearly discriminated against as women by both public and private institutions. This inequity must be a concern of both disabled sexes. In general disabled men are not the cause of this discriminatory treatment. Nonetheless, they cannot afford to ignore or tolerate this type of restriction, or they imitate those oppressors who take away rights for all disabled persons. As disabled women become more vocal in their demands they must not be told by those fighting able-bodism that to raise the issue of sexism will only "cloud" the issues or detract from the support of others outside of the group. Thus, there will be increasing, justified demands placed on disabled men to acknowledge the multiple minority status of disabled women and to refuse preferential treatment based on their sex. Since the disability movement is so new and has almost no documentation of its membership and leaders, it is difficult to know if sexism within the disabled rights movement is occurring. However, an awareness of this potential conflict of interest between disabled men and women may forestall the establishment of a male-based minority movement which can be expected in a sexist society.

There are parallel problems for disabled women in reference to their "dominant" minority groups. The sexism of the "helping" professions and institutions can produce more benefits for disabled men than for disabled women. Such differential treatment, however, is often a function of powerful institutions which provide limited opportunities for all disabled people. Both disabled men and women need to align for recognition of their basic rights, but disabled women must also fight for their special interests. These shared, particular disadvantages include not only battles against able-bodism and sexism, but additionally a recognition of the interaction effects of both minority statuses. These effects are examined more fully below.

Physically Disabled Women and Negative Interaction Effects

As noted above the problems of disabled women often run parallel to those of disabled males and able-bodied females, but there are additional interactive effects, unique to disabled women, that must be considered. One is the norm of passivity that is associated with both minority groups—the disabled and women. For disabled women, these attitudes interact, yielding exceedingly low expectations for achievement.

> Both groups are encouraged to be helpless, nonassertive, nonsexual, nonathletic, dependent, passive, grateful and apologetic for a less than perfect body in a society where physical appearance is often the measure of a value (Dailey, 1979: 41).

Another, similar interaction effect is the concern for appearance associated with women (Alta, 1973). For disabled women, a flaw in physical self-presentation may be exacerbated by limitations on physical mobility or strength (Dailey, 1979:42). This compounding effect, moreover, illustrates the tendency of one minority status to generate another.

A third interacting effect occurs when disabled women are considered unfeminine. There are numerous reasons why such perceptions could be generated. Because of their limited income, they may not be able to afford expensive clothing. Some disabled women also need custom-made clothing to accomodate non-standard body shapes and medical devices. In addition, their clothing choices may be restricted due to their physical limitations. This is particularly problematic when selecting footwear; e.g., high heels and sandals. Disabled women, too, may become very assertive and demanding because of the frequent infringement of their rights. This self-defense may be seen by others as behavior that is "unbecoming" to a woman. Women are generally more circumscribed in their speech and noverbal communication than are men (Goffman, 1976, 1977). In reference to gender-related speech, disabled women who speak too loudly because of sensory or speech disabilities may be subject to more extreme sanctions than disabled men with similar disabilities. In reference to gender-related body language, women who are unable to sit "decorously" or in "ladylike" positions because of physical limitations are similarly subjected to greater disapproval than their male counterparts.

Positive Effects

Simultaneously, some positive interaction effects could emerge from the freedom to recognize and therefore disregard able-bodism as a restrictive and narrow perspective. Thus, disabled women may concentrate on their work, dress comfortably, or be accepted as a friend, while some able-bodied women continue to struggle with sexist standards of appearance and beauty, have few career interests, or lack a sense of independence.

Disabled women are also less likely to be stigmatized for their physical limitations than disabled males. As a result, disabled women may be more at ease with the able-bodied female subculture than their disabled male counterparts. In other words, women are rarely socially stigmatized for lack of participation in sports or muscle development, while men may frequently be pressured to compete in sports, the military, or physically strenuous activities.

When a person is evaluated as "outside" of sexual competition, this has painful and important restrictions on one's sexuality. Concomitantly, this same competition can be demeaning and humiliating. Interaction based on a more egalitarian system of rules can open up new possibilities for relationships and sexual expression. Although sexual discrimination is unjust, disabled women can find an acceptance with men and women that is often difficult to achieve for the "able-bodied" or "attractive." (This phenomenon is similar to that found with the elderly or overweight who feel that they can say what they please because they are free of the constraints of conformity.)

Physically disabled women may develop particularly strong family ties with parents and siblings in a world where such ties are becoming increasingly attentuated. They may also form unusually close friendships with each other because they live in an overtly hostile and unappreciative environment.

Finally, those disabled women who do achieve success in their lives (whether in the marketplace, the home, or an institution) have fought a difficult battle and emerged triumphant. To generate a good life, especially against such extreme odds, is a remarkable achievement. This generates a strong sense of self and personal meaning. These disabled women, who may have some majority group identifications and resources, are simultaneously part of majority populations. These "majority" statuses cannot be overlooked when a list of "problems" is generated. For example, some disabled women are wealthy, while others are highly educated, or both. (Unfortunately, some may even be racist or homophobic.)

The positive effects of being both disabled and female can result in a sense of strength, understanding, compassion, and power that is rarely associated with disabled women. Becker has captured this reality when she writes:"We are first and foremost sensitive human beings with a terrific sense of accomplishment after all of the horrible, but challenging, experiences we have been through" (1977: xvi).

A disabled woman is clearly subjected to a broad range of social and economic constraints. She struggles against stigmatization and problems that are compounded by two minority statuses. Nonetheless, disabled women do survive and flourish in this restrictive environment. A totally negative analysis does not allow for a conceptual understanding of this human strength and potential.

Physically Disabled Women and Minority Relations: The Conclusion

There are clearly direct parallels between being disabled women, a multiple minority group, and being women or being disabled, where each of these last two groups comprise a single minority. Despite this commonality, there are some unique theoretical issues that confront the multiple minority group that distinguish them from their single minority counterparts. Perhaps comparisons on structural discrimination can be more fruitfully made between disabled women and Hispanic, aged women (see, for example, Stephens, Ostriker, and Blau, 1980) or between disabled women and lesbians, or between disabled women and Black Muslims. Almquist and Wehrle-Einhorn's work is notable in this regard (1978). They compare economic data on several groups of American minority women: blacks, American Indians, and groups of the following origins: Filipino, Chinese, Japanese, Puerto Rican, Mexican, and Cuban. By comparing incomes and occupations of these minority females with their respective minority males and then with Anglo females, they document that the patterns of discrimination for minority women are more similar to those of Anglo women than those of other minority men. Such an analysis could be extended to include physically disabled women. Another example illustrating the potential strengths of multiple minority comparisons and analyses can be seen in Hacker's work. Showing the usefulness of the minority perspective whether studying women (1951) or gay people (1971), her insights could be developed further by analyzing other, specific multiple minority groups. If such comparisons are made, we will know more about the phenomenon of multiple minority groups as well as analyzing which minority statuses are the most restrictive. There is a hierarchy of minority statuses, and this pattern interacts with the multiple minority status. In fact, this hierarchy may change when there is more than one minority status.

Adding this kind of complexity to minority analysis is important for understanding the process of discrimination and how to change it. At the present, many in-group and out-group identifications are very unidimensional, causing many people with some "majority" and "minority" statuses to be unaware of their common interests in oppressing others. The multiple minority group can become a mechanism for critiquing one minority's role in restricting others. This is particularly viable for a multiple minority's critique of a related "single" minority group, for the vested interests of a single minority group may be counter to those of the multiple minority members. An analysis of this differential interest may aid in articulating both common and separate concerns. Efforts to improve intergroup minority relations can also facilitate understanding of how to improve relations between themselves and other minority groups or the majority.

Information on multiple minority relations is needed to clarify the differential interest and problems of the minority and multiple minority. Emphasis on the general problems of competition and the divisiveness of single issue approaches is needed. Acceptance of the concepts of "winners" and "losers" forces minority groups to operate by the "rules" of the majority. If these processual definitions of *how* to gain one's rights are rejected, then the multiple minority group can draw upon the resources of other minority groups to aid in their struggles for recognition.

Out of this welter of identifications, it is possible that minority groups may see how very large a numerical majority they are. Instead of defining society as a massive, united, and anonymous force, it is more accurate to view social power and structure as complex, contradictory, and enacted by both anonymous others and those we know in everyday life. Instead of defining each minority as oppressed and restricted in opportunities by a large and unified majority, the pattern of such discrimination can be perceived as benefitting only a very small elite. This numerically tiny group benefits from the competition between disadvantaged groups. The dispossessed and second class citizens, because of their alienation and sense of isolation, allow themselves to be defined as in opposition with other disenfranchised groups. Minority groups often participate in each other's exploitation, as well as passively support control by the few. Discrimination in the marketplace, socialization, sexuality, and reproduction limits the lives of almost all members of our society. Only a small number of affluent, "beautiful", young, able-bodied, heterosexual, white males are allowed to fully entact the opportunities and dreams of this culture.

It is time for the minorities and multiple minorities to join interests and share visions of a world in which they are the community and they are the myth-makers.

Notes

1. I would like to thank Nancy Brooks and Michael Hill who made insightful comments on earlier drafts of this article. Special thanks is extended to the class members of the course "Women: the World's Minority" for their arguments, compassion, and hard work. This exploratory, innovative exchange was possible because of the open structure of Centennial College of the University of Nebraska. Unfortunately this college is now defunct due to budget cuts. The author takes final responsibility for this paper.
2. It must be noted that Hacker's insightful work on women as a minority group was not widely accepted until the past decade. Thus, the sexism of the profession and the significant change in social consciousness which have occurred since 1951 are both revealed. See Hacker (1975) for a discussion of these phenomena.
3. Sagrin's book precisely records the process of including more people within widening circles of self-reflective and disenfranchised group identifications (1975).

Jordan's article on the physically handicapped, published in the Sagrin collection, refutes the thesis of this article that the disabled are members of a minority group. He prefers to call them "disadvantaged" instead. His arguments are not accepted here because of the narrowness of his definition of the concept of "minority group." As noted above, Wirth and Hacker's definitions are used here. It is also worth noting that the literature on the disabled has been applying this concept of minority group to the disabled for a number of decades, although it has only become popularly accepted recently. See, for example, Barker (1948) and Wright (1960).

4. To adequately examine why new minority identifications are occurring with increasing frequency would require a separate article. This would include an analysis of social movements, the relationships between social movements, changes in legislation, changing demands for human and civil rights and altered awareness of unjust treatment. However, it is worth considering that there appears to be a "domino effect" with social rights movements. As one group challenges the system and protests injustice, other groups see the rightness and success of the former's demands and become aware of their own acceptance of group limits. Another possible explanation for this "chain reaction" could be "relative deprivation" theory. As one group improves their status, other groups become aware of their own disadvantaged status which may appear even lower after the granting of rights to another group.

5. Wilson's book, *On the Declining Significance of Race* (1978), documents the shifting class and race structure in the United States. He states that we are in a period of transition from racial to class inequalities with a large number of people who are poor and from numerous racial and ethnic groups. It is worth noting that a significant portion of the members of this underclass are women and their children.

6. Discrimination due to overweight is a more severe problem for women than for men. "Fat" is a sex-linked term, but truly obese men are subject to discriminatory treatment, too (Millman, 1980).

7. The whole issue of a black matriarchy is questioned by many black feminists: e.g. Stone (1970) and Higginbotham (1980).

8. "Sexism" is a prejudicial belief that women are socially less important, powerful, and desirable than men. "Able-bodism" is a prejudicial belief that people with physiological disabilities are socially less important, powerful, and desirable than people with bodies viewed as "normal." Both prejudicial beliefs are acted upon so that the structural opportunities and patterns of social interaction are systematically limited throughout society. Both discriminations are also based on myths associated with the body and in this way are philosophically linked.

References

Albrecht, G., ed. 1975. *Sociology of Physical Disability and Rehabilitation*. Pittsburgh: University of Pittsburgh Press.

Almquist, E. J., and J. L. Wehrle-Einhorn. 1978. "The doubly disadvantaged: Minority women in the labor force." In A. Stromberg and S. Harkess, eds. *Women Working*. Palo Alto, Calif.: Mayfield . Pp. 63-88.

Alta. 1971. "Pretty." In V. Gornick and B. Moran, eds. *Woman in a Sexist Society*. New York: Basic Books. Pp. 35-36.

Barker, R. G. et al. 1948. *Adjustment to Physical Handicap and Illness*. Bulletin 55, 2d edition. New York: Social Science Research Council.

de Beauvoir, S. 1970. *The Second Sex*. New York: Bantam Books (c. 1949).

Becker, E. F. 1978. *Female Sexuality Following Spinal Cord Injury*. Bloomington, Ill.: Chaever.

Cook, L and A. Rossett. 1975. "The sex role attitude of deaf adolescent women and their implications for vocational choice." *American Annals of the Deaf* 120: 341-45.

Cotera, M. 1980. "Feminism: The Chicana and the Anglo versions." In M. Melville, ed. *Twice a Minority*. St. Louis: C. V. Mosby. Pp. 217-34.

Dailey, A. L. T. 1979. "Physically handicapped women." *Counseling Psychologist* 8: 41-42.

Daly, M. 1978. *Gyn/Ecology*. Boston: Beacon Press.

Epstein, C. F. 1973. "Positive effects of the multiple negative." *American Journal of Sociology* 78: 912-35.

Freeman, Jo, ed. 1979. *Women: A Feminist Perspective*, 2d edition. Palo Alto, Cal.: Mayfield.

Gillespie, P. H. and A. H. Fink. 1974. "The influence of sexism on the education of handicapped children." *Exceptional Children* 41: 155-62.

Goffman, E. 1977. "The arrangement between the sexes." *Theory and Society* 4: 301-31.

———. 1976. "Gender display, 'picture frames,' and 'gender commercials'." In E. Goffman. *Gender Advertisements. Studies in the Anthropology of Visual Communication*. Vol. 3, no. 2: 69-95.

Hacker, H. M. 1975. "Women as minority group twenty years later". In R. K. Unger and F. L. Denmark, eds. *Women: Dependent or Independent Variable?* New York: Psychological Dimensions, Inc. Pp. 103-15.

———. 1971. "Homosexuals: Deviant or minority group?" In E. Sagrin, ed. *The Other Minorities*. Waltham, Mass: Xerox Publishing. Pp. 65-92.

———. 1951. "Woman as a minority group." *Social Forces* 30: 60-69.

Higginbotham, E. 1980. "Issues in contemporary sociology work on Black women." *Humanity and Society* 4: 226-42.

Howe, L. K. 1977. *Pink Collar Workers: Inside the World of Women's Work*. New York: Avon Books.

Huber, J., ed. 1973. *Changing Women in a Changing Society*. Chicago: University of Chicago Press.

Jordan, S. 1963. "The disadvanataged group: A concept applicable to the physically handicapped." *Journal of Psychology* 55: 313-22.

Kent, D. 1977. "In search of liberation." *Disabled U.S.A.* 3: 18-19.

Kolodny, R. C. 1972. "Sexual dysfunction in diabetic females." *Medical Aspects of Human Sexuality* 6: 98-106.

Lewis, D. 1977. "A response to inequality: Black women, racism and sexism." *Signs* 3: 339-61.

———. 1975. "The Black family: Socialization and sex roles." *Phylon* 36: 221-37.

Markson, E. W. and B. Hess. 1980. "Older women in the city." *Signs* 5, supplement: 127-43.

Millman, M. 1980. *Such a Pretty Face: Being Fat in America*. New York: W. W. Norton.

O'Toole, J. C. and C. Weeks. 1978. *What Happened After School? A study of Disabled Women's Education Equity Communications Network*. San Francisco: Far West Laboratory for EducationalResearch and Development.

Park, R. E. 1926. "Our racial frontier on the Pacific." *Survey Graphic* 56: 192-96.

Reich, M., D. M. Gordon, and R. C. Edwards. 1973. "A theory of labor market segmentation." *Economic Review* 63: 359-65.

Rose, P. I. 1965. *They and We: Racial and Ethnic Relations in the United States.* New York: Random House.

Safilios-Rothschild, C. 1972. *Toward a Sociology of Women.* Lexington, Mass.: Xerox College .

———. 1970. *The Sociology and Social Psychology of Disability and Rehabilitation.* New York: Random House.

Stephens, R. C., G. T. Oser and Z. S. Blau. 1980. "To be aged, Hispanic, and female: The triple risk." In M. Melville, ed. *Twice a Minority.* St. Louis: C. V. Mosby.Pp. 249-58.

Stone, P. T. 1975. "Feminist consciousness and Black women." In J. Freeman, ed. *Women: A Feminist Perspective*, 2d edition. Palo Alto, Calif.: Mayfield Publishing Company. Pp. 575-88.

U.S. Department of Commerce. 1981. *Money Income of Families and Persons in the United States.* Bureau of the Census, Current Population Reports. Washington, D.C.: U.S. Government Printing Office.

Wagley, C. and M. Harris. 1958. *Minorities in the New World: Six Case Studies.* New York: Columbia University Press.

Wilson, W. J. 1978. *The Declining Significance of Race.* Chicago: University of Chicago Press.

Wirth, L. 1945. "The problems of minority groups." In R. Linton, ed. *The Science of Man in the World Crisis.* New York: Columbia University Press. Pp. 347-72.

Wright, B. A. 1960. *Physical Disabilities—A Psychological Approach.* New York: Harper Brothers.

Yetman, N. R. and C. H. Steele, eds. 1971. *Majority and Minority: The Dynamics of Racial and Ethnic Relations.* Boston: Allyn and Bacon.

5

Sex Role Attitudes and Role Reorganization in Spinal Cord Injured Women

Emily Bonwich

Traumatic spinal cord injuries require massive re-training for both physical and social skills. Traditionally, the literature on spinal cord injuries has stressed the importance of the male's role more than the female's. This paper examines the changes in role and feminine self-concept experienced by rural women as an exploratory step in filling the gaps in our understanding of this traumatic physical injury.

Introduction

Traumatic spinal cord injury is one of the most extreme forms of stress in human experience. Without warning or preparation the body is paralyzed. Suddenly the person is dependent on others for routine bodily functions and must slowly and painfully relearn the simplest of physical skills. New skills must be acquired to replace those that have been lost forever. Destruction of self-esteem, disintegration of intimate relationships, and loss of social role can be additional consequences of the severe physical disability.

Studies of the psychosocial consequences of spinal cord injury have focused primarily upon the needs and problems of men. This is partly because the injury occurs far more often to men (in a ratio of over four to one), but it is also because of the widespread belief that women in general adjust better to physical disability than do men. For example, it has long been thought that women's roles in society are not as severely limited by the wheelchair as are men's roles. The traditional view of sex roles holds that dependency and passivity are more natural for females than for males. A woman, even if disability requires that she use a wheelchair, can still manage a household, direct others in household tasks, provide emotional support to a family, and function sexually in a "relatively passive" manner. Such traditionally female

56

role activities, though they require more effort after spinal cord injury, can still be performed in a way that conforms to society's expectations because they are primarily expressive. Men, on the other hand, traditionally have been expected to perform instrumental roles, ones which required strength, physical activity, manipulation, and mobility in the world outside the home.[1] They are also expected to be aggressive in the act of sex. Because spinal cord injury makes some of these activities impossible and seriously impedes others, it is felt that male self-esteem and sex role identity are seriously threatened (Christopherson, 1968). If it is true that women can more comfortably accept dependence upon parents or husband because society does not expect much more of them, then they have less need to be mobile outside the home in order to fulfill their destinies and find personal satisfaction. If women's roles are expected to be primarily supportive or "expressive," then they can more easily be performed despite limits on physical mobility caused by spinal cord injury than can masculine, aggressive, "instrumental" roles. Such were the conclusions of studies appearing in the literature of 10 to 20 years ago (Deutsch and Goldston, 1960; Weiss and Diamond, 1966; Fink, Skipper and Hallenbeck, 1968).

Despite broad, societal changes in beliefs and values regarding the roles of women, despite the double standard of physical attractiveness that has existed since ancient times, despite the overwhelming evidence that women experience more physical and mental ill health than men (the latter often attributed to the greater strains inherent in their social role obligations), such beliefs continue to circulate in rehabilitation literature (cf. Levitt, 1980). To the extent that they are incorrect or misleading, they may seriously interfere with the provision of appropriate services to patients.

The critical fact is that there is a scarcity of empirical data on the effects of spinal cord injury on the lives of women. Spinal cord injured women attempting to rebuild their lives after their injuries may well be caught in a double bind. If they are women who characteristically play the independent assertive roles advocated by the women's movement, after spinal cord injury a monumental struggle to regain independence and control over their lives must begin. Obstacles to be overcome in terms of employment, mobility and financial self-sufficiency are no less imposing than those that are faced by men. In fact, women may have to overcome sex discrimination in addition to prejudice against the handicapped.[2]

On the other side of the coin are women's traditional roles referred to in the literature—emotionally expressive, dependent, and nurturant. Is it really logical to perceive women whose roles fit this pattern as having an easier time than men in adjusting to spinal cord injury? On the contrary. For women with traditional values, the double standard of attractiveness and social desirability imposed by society can be especially cruel. A psychiatrist deploring the fate of "the unattractive woman" observed that men do not have to be physically attractive to succeed in life because they are judged as much on personality, intelligence, and achievement as on conformity to standards of physical perfection (Seidenberg, 1973). Men have imposed standards of social worth on females that they do not apply to themselves. Unfortunately, many women accept these standards as their own and evaluate themselves as well as other females in terms of current "body beautiful" norms.

Fine and Asch (see Chapter 2 in this book) cited research showing that disabled women are more likely to be deserted by their spouses after injury than are disabled men. Disabled women are also less likely to marry than are able-bodied women, perhaps, according to Fine and Asch, because they are assumed to be inappropriate mothers or sex objects. A woman aware of such prejudices will almost certainly have difficulty reconciling her self-image after disability with traditional concepts of femininity. One could speculate that spinal cord injured women who recognize this double bind would change their definition of their roles as part of the process of adjustment. Not only are major role changes likely to be imposed on women without their volition as a consequence of the injury, but women may actively seek and bring about such changes as a coping mechanism.

The purpose of this article is to report some findings from an exploratory study of changes in role and feminine self-concept among spinal cord injured women from a predominantly rural culture. It was felt that information about rural spinal cord injured women was needed to supplement that which had been obtained from interviews with well educated urban samples (Fitting et al., 1978; Bregman and Hadley, 1976; Becker, 1978) and to identify issues of female self-perception, relationships and roles that had hitherto been neglected.

Data were primarily qualitative, obtained in informal semi-structured interviews with 36 spinal cord injured women who were from one to 26 years post injury. Role reorganization was assessed by a series of open-ended questions asking the respondent to compare her major life roles before the injury with those she performed after the injury. (Also explored were feelings about self, femininity, sexuality, problems of marital and other partner relationships, the family, and community involvement.) Sex role attitudes were assessed by means of a quantitative measure, the Brogan-Kutner Sex Role Orientation Scale (Brogan and Kutner, 1976). The scale contains 36 statements expressing beliefs and values regarding appropriate roles for men and women in society, division of labor in marriage, child rearing, social power structure, and occupational choice. The respondent indicated the extent of her agreement or disagreement with each statement on a Likert scale. Scores are then summed to produce an overall Sex Role Orientation (SRO) Score, which enables differentiation among individuals with relatively traditional attitudes and those with relatively nontraditional or "liberated" attitudes.

Results

The ages of the women interviewed ranged from 19 to 69 years. Eleven women had not completed high school, 14 were high school graduates, 6 had attended one or two years of college, and 5 had college degrees or postgraduate education. Fifteen women were single (had never been married), 12 women were married (two of these were not living with their husbands), 7 women were divorced, 1 was widowed, and 1 reported her status as separated. Seventeen of the women were mothers; 3 had borne children after the injury. Fifteen (42 percent) women were paraplegic, 14 (39 percent) were quadriplegic, and 7 (18 percent) had been paralyzed but had recovered the ability to walk, despite some residual motor and sensory impairment.

Many women we interviewed had experienced lasting role changes as a result of their injuries. The kinds of changes they reported are listed in Table 5.1 and will be discussed in more detail below.

One of the most serious blows to the self is the loss of a loved one (Jacobs and Ostfeld, 1977), and when a primary relationship is broken an important social role is lost as well. Twenty-nine of the women interviewed were married or were involved in a serious romantic relationship when their injury occurred. Of these intense primary relationships 15, or over half, were dissolved, in the view of the respondents, because of the injury. Seven women stated that

TABLE 5.1
Role Reorganization Attributed by Subjects to Injury

	Number of Women
Lost husband or lover	15
Lost custody of children	5
Gave up plans to have children	8
Lost abilities to work at valued former occupation	9
Multiple valued role losses	9
Gained education	5
Gained career opportunity	5
Gained financial independence through aid to disabled	4
Gained new husband or long-term relationship	2
Multiple role gains	4

their marriages were destroyed because of the injury—even if they themselves precipitated the separation—for reasons like: "Because he couldn't take it," "I knew he wanted out," "He didn't want a cripple." One woman said: "He acted like he didn't want to be bothered when I had to ask him for help. He hated to have me dependent on him. He wanted me to be the strong one in the marriage." The other eight women also reported that a significant love relationship was lost. One woman still lives with her boyfriend, but their planned marriage was called off and she stated that she won't marry him as long as she must be in a wheelchair. Three women, now walking and whose relationships have remained intact, volunteered the information that they never would have agreed to marry their husbands or remained in their marriages if they had not eventually regained the ability to walk. Women often seemed to feel that they had no right to keep an able-bodied man "tied down" to a woman in a wheelchair. "It would not be fair" said one respondent. Some women, too, seemed unwilling to remain physically and emotionally dependent on a man, and thereby be vulnerable to his rejection. If they were first to reject a partner or potential partner then they would protect themselves from the inevitable hurt. As one woman revealed:

> I broke off the engagement (I think he was secretly relieved). He was afraid of hurting me sexually. His passion was so strong he was not sure he could be faithful. I was afraid I would be jealous and insecure as the years went by. If I put all my eggs in one basket—marriage—I would be overly vulnerable to someone else taking him away.

After the experience of breaking off an intimate romantic relationship, several women repudiated the possibility of any such relationship for themselves in the future that would make them dependent, speaking of not wanting to need a man ever again. For some it involved struggling to overcome sexual impulses as well as feelings of weakness and loneliness. Other women went on to have several new relationships while at the same time trying to develop new strength and independence in themselves. After these positive experiences they were able to view the loss of the lover or husband they were with at the time of the injury as "good riddance" of a mate who was never worthy of them in the first place.

Another painful loss occurred for some women when they gave up the maternal role. Of 17 women who had children at the time of the injury, five relinquished custody of their children because they could not take care of them. In three cases the husband took the children away at the time of separation. Eight childless women said the injury forced them to give up their plans to have children, not for medical reasons, but because physical and financial limitations would make it too difficult to care for children, especially when small. Another married woman said that she wanted children but had none because she and her husband discontinued sexual relations after the injury due to her loss of sensation during intercourse.

For a person who has been a member of the work force, with regular, paid employment outside the home, discontinuing work activity represents a very real role loss. For spinal cord injured women, employment options are few, just as they are for men. Not only are job opportunities limited in the small towns where most of our subjects live, but the small communities usually lag behind in providing accessibility in the work place, in public facilities, and transportation. All but five of the 36 women in this study had worked before injury and 21 were fully self-supporting. Only eight are working full time now. Employment provides not only income but also social contacts and structure to daily life. Loss of the work role might be expected to have negative effects on self-esteem and life satisfaction. On the whole, however, our interview subjects did not perceive these losses as major problems.[3] Nine women did state that they would like very much to find employment, but were hampered by the lack of opportunity and transportation in their home towns. It is likely that many of the women in our study who worked before injury did so to supplement the family income rather than to pursue a lifetime career, and thus did not consider the loss of this particular role as the most distressing.

Although over half of the women who were in an intimate relationship at the time of injury lost that loved person, when asked what they "missed most" since the injury, loss of a relationship was seldom named. None of the women stated that sexual activity was the thing they missed most. As found in interviews with spinal cord injured men (Hansen and Franklin, 1976), our respondents usually named physical activities they could no longer perform—walking, sports, running—and general freedom of mobility as things they missed most. Physical limitations seemed to be the most salient consequence of the injury, a fact that is not surprising in light of the extent to which physical limitations affect other aspects of life. However, since many women had expressed bitterness, heartache and sadness earlier in the interview as they described disrupted relationships, it is evident those were deeply felt losses.

Loss, whether of relationships and obligations, familiar routines, or important gratifications, severely strains the individual's psychological coping resources. Our interviews revealed how frequently, for women, other losses compounded the supreme insult of spinal cord injury. Not just one but many events conspired to produce stress and require readjustment. It is remarkable that most women appeared reasonably successful in the coping tasks that confronted them.

Twelve of our interview subjects were able to identify major positive changes that had taken place in their lives as a result of the injury. Despite having lost important roles and relationships, new roles had been acquired that became the focus of their self-identities. It is as if the spinal cord injury had a shattering effect on a woman's traditional role expectations for herself and provided the stimulus for liberation from constraints imposed by feminine sex role stereotypes. A typical quote is, "What my body can do is limited since the spinal cord injury but my spirit is freer now". When such a positive role reorganization occurred it had two consequences: First, the woman was performing roles that she never had imagined for herself before the injury and that in her opinion would have been highly unlikely in her former social and cultural setting. (Because they occurred after the injury and were attributed to the injury, they can be conceptualized as "role gains.") Second, these women had greatly increased self-esteem, partly as a result of having mastered demanding new roles (often of a higher status) and partly as a result of having overcome formidable obstacles to do so. As Skipper and his associates (1968) noted, coping with the hardships of disability may indeed be a self-actualizing activity.

Such positive changes in self-concept could be related to traditional norms of femininity, attractiveness, and sexuality. Some women in the group with positive new roles did not think that their images of themselves as women had greatly changed. Their expression of sexuality was essentially the same as it had been before, in its importance in their lives and in the degree of pleasure it afforded. They rated themselves as about as attractive now as before the injury and their efforts to enhance their physical appearance had not changed. That is, their use of makeup and attention to hair style and clothing after the injury was similar to their custom before the injury. Other women considered themselves *more attractive* as women than they were before their spinal cord injury. These women often said that they now had different ideas about what a woman's role should be, giving less importance to conventional wife-mother roles and "man pleasing" attributes than to their own self-actualization and accomplishments.

All women with positive role reorganization identified changes in themselves of the sort commonly referred to as "character". For instance, they were likely to say that they now have "more inner strength," more "guts"; they have a better ability to get along with people because they are more compassionate; they are broader in outlook and more tolerant than before. A frequent remark was, "I like myself better now than I did before I was injured." Taken as a whole, the 12 women who reported positive role reorganization were less traditional in sex role attitudes than the rest of the sample. This was indicated by the higher mean score of this group on the Sex Role Orientation Scale (Table 5.2). Women who reported that they definitely had developed a more positive feminine self-concept since the injury also appeared to have less traditional attitudes (Table 5.3).

TABLE 5.2
Role Reorganization and Sex Role Orientation Score

	N	Mean SRO Score
One or more new roles	12	172.8
No new roles	23	164.7

TABLE 5.3
Change in Feminine Self Concept and Sex Role Orientation Score

Change in Self Concept	N	Mean SRO Score*
No change	16	163.8
More positive	6	176.3
Less positive	13	167.6
Total	35	

*The higher the sex role orientation score the more nontraditional the attitude toward women's roles.

Several women from rural communities reported that it was rehabilitation counseling while they were hospitalized that had opened new horizons to them. Had the spinal cord injury not occurred, and had they not received comprehensive rehabilitation services in a major center, they would have aspired to little beyond marriage and motherhood roles. "I would have been a farm wife with 12 kids," declared one woman who obtained a college degree and professional certification after her injury. She believes that she probably will eventually marry—she has refused two proposals since her injury—but she feels no pressure to be married in order to fulfill a female role. Her professional role provides the independent income, travel opportunities, and social contact she might not have had otherwise. Five women in this group were receiving Department of Vocational Rehabilitation support to attend college or technical training schools at the time they were interviewed.

Over half of the subjects were receiving some form of insurance compensation or assistance for the disabled. For four women this check was their first experience with money to spend at their own discretion, and they considered that they had thereby gained a measure of independence. For others, the assistance check was only a partial substitute for their own earnings or support from their husbands prior to the injury, and thus could not be considered as contributing to a positive role change or improvement in status of any kind.

During the interview the subjects were asked what one thing they liked best about themselves now compared with before the injury. Traits the women named fell into four categories: traits related to independence and autonomy (such as, "I am a strong person"); traits related to successful interpersonal relationships, ("I'm more outgoing now—I like people more"); traits related to a traditional nurturant role ("I am a good mother"); and a miscellaneous category. The women who named nurturant traits had a markedly lower mean sex role orientation score, indicating that they were likely to have traditional attitudes. Those who named traits related to independence and interpersonal relationships were more nontraditional (Table 5.4).

Discussion

Traditional sex role stereotypes place a negative value on many traits believed to be typical of females. The stereotypes promote belief in the inferior competence of women and limit the social role choices available as a means to fulfillment of individual needs and capacities. A basic tenent of the women's movement is that nontraditional sex role attitudes have beneficial effects on the lives of women (and men) in many circumstances. This perspective has been the foundation for consciousness-raising efforts, organization of female support groups, assertiveness training, and many other activities directed toward attitude and behavior change. Although these values have become incorporated into the ideology of helping professions, it is difficult to find empirical research to support them.

Felton and her associates (1980) concluded from a study of women and men undergoing marital counseling that nontraditional sex role attitudes were

TABLE 5.4
Traits Subjects Liked Best about Themselves and Sex Role Orientation Score

Best Self	N	Mean SRO Score
Independence	13	183.8
Relational	10	184.2
Nurturance	10	129.8
Other	2	166.5
Total	35	

a coping resource for women in these circumstances because they reduced distress in response to marital difficulties. As we have seen, spinal cord injury often results in the loss of former roles for women. In order to adjust, women may need to assume new roles that do not fall within stereotyped sex role patterns. Nontraditional sex role attitudes provide increased psychological flexibility and freedom of choice with regard to new roles. A woman need not feel a sense of failure and guilt at being unable or unwilling to meet the requirements of traditional feminine roles. Other potential sources of self-esteem become viable alternatives.

Deegan (see Chapter 4 in this volume) pointed out in her discussion of disabled women as members of a multiple minority group that being twice discriminated against can have positive interaction effects. For example, being considered outside of sexual or occupational competition provides a certain freedom from conventional expectations for behavior. Disabled women some-times find a degree of acceptance with other women and with men that is partly a result of their being perceived as nonthreatening. They may also be more free to pursue individual goals without the constraints of conformity to restrictve sex-role standards. The presence of nontraditional sex role attitudes and values would appear, from the reports of women in this study, to be a major factor in enabling women to capitalize on their individual strengths, to increase their self esteem, and to learn new roles.

If these values were acquired during the rehabilitation process, there are important implications for the professions working with assertiveness training and other behavior change methods. In helping any spinal cord injured person through the rehabilitation process, all possible coping resources must be strengthened. Since nontraditional sex role attitudes may be a particularly effective psychological coping resource for women, women should be pro-vided with opportunities to explore non traditional roles for themselves and to develop nontraditional sources of self-esteem. A spinal cord injured woman should be encouraged to take the initial risks required in trying out her new image as she relates to friends and loved ones and in making new acquaint-ances. This demands a great deal of patience and support from rehabilitation staff. At the same time women whose self-concepts are deeply rooted in traditional female roles need to be provided with emotional support and un-derstanding when they experience conflicts between their habit of dependence and the rehabilitation institution's demand that they work toward greater independence. It is important to remain nonjudgmental regarding value sys-tems and individual preferences different from our own.

The importance of sexual and relationship counseling for spinal cord injured women cannot be overstated. Contrary to the general clinical impression, spinal cord injured women do have significant problems in these areas and perhaps many can be alleviated through counseling that recognizes their special needs. A number of interview studies in addition to our own have indicated that spinal cord injured women do not feel they were adequately informed about their sexuality during their rehabilitation (Glass and Padrone, 1978; Becker, 1978; Comarr and Virgue, 1978). Sexual functioning is a major concern because it is a source of self-esteem for both traditional and nontraditional women.

It cannot be determined conclusively from a study of this design, which depends on subjects' self-reports of past and present attitudes, that women who seize the lemon that life has handed them and "make lemonade," were less conservative and traditional before the disaster struck or whether, as they gradually developed strengths and broader experiences, they changed in that direction. A longitudinal study of sex role attitudes from shortly after injury through long-term follow-up would provide more information. It should also be possible to test the function of nontraditional sex role attitudes as a coping resource for spinal cord injured women by administering a scale that measures psychological distress.

What our exploratory study has demonstrated is that traumatic spinal cord injury represents an overwhelming attack on the pattern of a woman's life, just as it does on a man's. Because the role strains are different for women, they are no less deserving of efforts to understand them and to provide the most appropriate assistance.

Notes

1. Concepts describing classic role distinctions as "expressive" and "instrumental" are found in T. Parsons and R. F. Bales, *Family, Socialization, and Interaction Process*. Glencoe: The Free Press, 1955. The work of Freud also supports this perspective.
2. Deegan (Chapter 4 in this volume) effectively argues that disabled women are members of a "multiple minority group" in that two socially devalued statuses— that of being disabled and that of being female—interact to place them in a doubly disadvantaged position.
3. Kutner and Kutner (1979) studied losses attributed to disability by patients hospitalized with a variety of disabling conditions. The 38 women in their sample stated, as did the men interviewed, that they missed most the "ability to work at job or housework." Many of the Kutners' subjects differed from ours in cultural and racial characteristics, on disability type, and probably on age as well. These factors may explain their different findings.

References

Becker, E. 1978. *Female Sexuality Following Spinal Cord Injury*. Bloomington, Ill: Accent.

Bregman, S. and R. Hadley. 1976. "Sexual adjustment and feminine attractiveness among spinal cord injured women." *Archives of Physical Medicine and Rehabilitation* 57: 448-50.

Brogan, D. and N. Kutner. 1976. "Measuring sex role orientation." *Journal of Marriage and the Family* 38: 29-40.

Christopherson, V. A. 1968. "Role modifications of the disabled male." *American Journal of Nursing* 68: 290-93.

Comarr, A. E. and M. S. Virgue. 1978. "Sexual counseling among male and female patients with spinal cord and/or Cauda Equina injury, Part II." *American Journal of Physical Medicine* 57: 215-27.

Deutsch, C. P. and J. A. Goldston. 1960. "Family factors in home adjustment of the severely disabled." *Marriage and Family Living* 22: 312-16.

Felton, B. J., P. Brown, S. Lehman, and P. Liberator. 1980. "The coping function of sex-role attitudes during marital disruption." *Journal of Health and Social Behavior* 21: 240-48.

Fink, S. L., J. K. Skipper and P. N. Hallenbeck. 1968. "Physical disability and problems in marriage." *Journal of Marriage and the Family* 30: 64-73.

Fitting, M., S. Salisbury, N. Daviews, and D. Mayclin. 1978. "Self-concept and sexuality of spinal cord injured women." *Archives of Sexual Behavior* 7: 1453-46.

Glass, D. and F. Padrone. 1978. "Sexual adjustment in the handicapped." *Journal of Rehabilition* 44: 43-47.

Hanson, R. W. and M. R. Franklin. 1976. "Sexual loss in relation to other functional losses for spinal cord injured males." *Archives of Physical Medicine and-Rehabilitation* 57: 291-3.

Jacobs, S. and A. M. Ostfield. 1977. "An epidemiological review of the mortality of bereavement." *Psychosomatic Medicine* 39: 344-57.

Kutner, N. and M. J. Kutner. 1979. "Race and sex as variables affecting reaction to disability." *Archives of Physical Medicine and Rehabilitation* 60: 62-66.

Levitt, R. 1980. "Understanding sexuality and spinal cord injury." *Journal of Neurosurgical Nursing* 12: 88-89.

Parsons, T. and R. F. Bales. 1955. *The Family, Socialization, and Interaction Process.* Glencoe: The Free Press.

Seidenberg, R. 1973. "Psychosocial adjustment of the unattractive woman." *Medical Aspects of Human Sexuality* 7: 60-81.

Skipper, J. K., S. L. Fink, and P. N. Hallenbeck. 1968. "Physical disability among married women: Problems in the husband-wife relationship." *Journal of Rehabilitation* 34: 16-19.

Weiss, A. and M. Diamond. 1966. "Sexual adjustment, identification, and attitudes of patients with myelopathy." *Archives of Physical Medicine and Rehabilitation* 47: 245-50.

6

Benefits for the Disabled: How Beneficial for Women?

Elizabeth Ann Kutza

The social and economic consequence of disability is of increasing interest in American society today. The number of persons reporting disabling conditions is rising, as is the number of persons qualifying for public disability benefits. This article examines the impact of current United States disability policy on disabled women, and concludes that the major programs—disability insurance, supplemental security income, workers' compensation, vocational rehabilitation—because of their relationship to labor market participation, disadvantage women. Women not only receive fewer but also less generous benefits. Explanations of this outcome and implications for future policy are addressed.

Introduction

The 1980's are likely to bring with them increased attention to the social and economic consequences of disability. Already this concern has been exhibited nationally through the convening of the 1977 White House Conference on Handicapped Individuals, and internationally through the designation of 1981 as the International Year of Disabled Persons. The highly symbolic political attention to the circumstances of disability in the American polity has emerged from three sources. One is the public's increased awareness of the extent of disability in our society, another is the increased cost associated with public and private disability benefits, and a third is the increased demands of the disabled themselves.

Not until the 1970 census was there any systematic attempt to identify the number of disabled persons living in the United States. The Census counted 11.2 million persons between the ages of 16 and 64 (one in eleven persons) with functional disabilities. Of this number, approximately 1.7 million persons were homebound due to chronic health disorders or degenerative diseases, and 2.1 million were institutionalized (President's Committee on Employment of the Handicapped, 1977). In 1972, the Social Security Administration conducted its Survey of Disabled and Nondisabled Adults, and counted one in nine persons disabled (15.6 million persons between the ages of 20 and 64) including approximately 7.7 million severely disabled (Allan, 1976).

Those first attempts at enumeration, however, have been criticized as underestimating the numbers of disabled persons in the U.S. The disability classification used in both surveys is based upon the individual's capacity to work. Those whose health prevents or limits them from working are classified as disabled. But many disabled persons do work, hence their disability is not an impediment to employment. Such persons, as well as persons over age 64, are omitted from counts of the disabled by the census and the Social Security Administration surveys.

Responding to the limitations of these studies by expanding the concept of disability, two alternate estimates of the number of disabled in our society have been put forth. The White House Conference on Handicapped Individuals estimated that 33 million persons living in the United Sates have physical or developmental disabilities, while the American Coalition of Citizens with Disabilities estimates the number at 36 million—one in six persons. Thus, the sheer number of persons having some handicapping condition has alerted policymakers and the public to the needs of this group.

While it is not absolutely certain whether physical and developmental disabilities among adults are on the rise in American society (since most enumerating attempts have been so recent), it is apparent that the number of persons who qualify for public benefits on the basis of disability is increasing. The numbers of workers who qualified for Social Security disability insurance benefits, for example, has doubled in seven years. The cost of the program has quadrupled since 1970 (Singer, 1978). Under the supplemental security income program, too, benefit receipt contingent upon disability is the fastest growing component. Workers' compensation and state vocational rehabilitation programs also are experiencing rapid growth. (Between 1975 and 1979, workers' compensation benefit outlays increased from $4.6 to $8.5 billion.)

Many provisions of the programs themselves have contributed to these increases, but the experiences of privately financed disability plans and of government programs in other countries generally have paralleled those of federal and state programs. Hence one conclusion might be that the public acceptance of the government's role in compensating for the functional limitations brought about by disability is growing. In 1979, federal benefit outlays for the disabled were estimated at totaling $35 billion (U.S. Office of Management and Budget, 1979). These growing budgetary outlays naturally have brought public disability programs increased—and often unwelcome—attention from national policymakers. And this attention predictably will continue.

A final impetus to the public concern about disability has come from the disabled themselves. Increased militancy by advocates of the disabled has generated new programs and placed new demands on policymakers. The disabled are striving to achieve mainstreaming in education, barrier-free environments, special transportation facilities, and equal access rules. Exercising their political muscle, the disabled have witnessed mixed results. While new programs are being developed, the budgetary implications of these demands are generating alarm and resistance at all levels of government.

Three factors, then, are combining to propel social policies for the disabled into the forefront of our national agenda for the 1980s. As existing programs undergo new scrutiny, it is appropriate to ask how their benefits affect disabled women. This article will explore the impact on disabled women of current United States policy for disabled persons.

Programs That Benefit the Disabled

Programs aimed at assisting the disabled have a long historical tradition. The lame, as they were earlier called, were regarded along with the aged and children as unable to fully participate in the economic activity of society. Because this inability to contribute was involuntary and unchanging, such individuals were seen as deserving of support by the larger collectivity. Resources generated by the able-bodied were transferred to the lame individual as part of a social contract. In early societies this transfer of resources occurred informally through family or clan; in more developed industrialized societies this collective responsibility has shifted to the formal organizations of government through the implementation of public policies.

Currently there is a wide range of benefits available to disabled individuals through public programs. Most of these programs are administered and funded by the federal government. Official government estimates identify more than 120 programs and activities serving handicapped individuals sponsored by 20 federal departments (U.S. Department of Health, Education, and Welfare, 1978a). Several of these programs provide services to children or the aged, but the majority of public policies that concern themselves with disability are directed to working-age adults. The major purpose of these programs is either to replace earnings lost through disability, or to provide services that rehabilitate handicapped persons so they may reenter the labor force and become self-sufficient. The four most significant programs are the disability insurance program under social security (DI); the supplemental security income program (SSI), the state workers' compensation and vocational rehabilitation programs.

Disability Insurance Under Social Security

The social insurance features of United States Social Security policy, embodied in Title II of the Social Security Act, provide for the partial replacement of earnings lost to workers and their dependents because of the worker's retirement in old age (old age insurance), disability severe enough to prevent substantial gainful employment (disability insurance), or death (survivors' insurance). Disability insurance pays wage-related benefits to the worker, the worker's children, and the caretaker (usually the mother) of the children of the disabled worker. In December 1982, the disability insurance cash benefit program provided monthly benefits to about 2.6 million disabled workers.

While now an integral part of the social security system, disability insurance provisions were enacted 21 years after the retirement program, and 17 years after enactment of survivors' insurance. "The delay," in the words of the 1979 Advisory Council on Social Security, "was the result, in part, of fears that providing social security disability benefits would discourage rehabilitation and encourage malingering, and that the costs of disability insurance would be difficult to control" (U.S. Advisory Council on Social Security, 1979, p. 139). These fears led to the adoption of a very limited disability insurance program in 1956. Only persons aged 50 and over were eligible for benefits. By 1960, benefit eligibility was liberalized, and coverage under DI began to parallel coverage under the old age and survivors' insurance provisions.

Benefit entitlement and benefit eligibility continued to liberalize in the 1960's and 1970's, and by 1975 the number of workers being awarded disability benefits was roughly twice its 1965 level. After 1975, however, the number of new awards declined, although benefit outlays continued to rise. Recent legislative proposals have been aimed at curtailing these continually rising costs.

Eligibility for disability insurance benefits are contingent upon three things: (1) insured status, (2) disability status, and (3) age. A worker must be 64 years of age or younger, and have a required number of quarters of coverage to be fully insured under the program. For fully insured status, a worker must have 20 quarters of coverage in the 40 quarters preceding the onset of his/her disability. (A quarter of coverage is a calendar quarter in which the individual receives wages of $50 or more.) In effect, than, at the time of his/her disability, an individual would have to have contributed to the social security system at least 5 of the preceding 10 years.

In addition to fully insured status, an indiviudal must fit the statutory definition of disability to be eligible for benefits. In the Social Security Act and its regulations, disability is defined as "the inability to engage in any substantial gainful activity by reason of any medically determinable physical or mental impairment which can be expected to last for a continuous period of not less than 12 months. A person must be not only unable to do his/her previous work or work commensurate with the previous work . . . but cannot, considering age, education, and work experience, engage in any other kind of substantial gainful work which exists in the national economy'' (U.S. Department of Health, Education, and Welfare, 1974). Under current regulations, earnings of more than $300 a month for 9 months are assumed to demonstrate an ability to engage in ''substantial gainful activity'' (SGA), and thus result in a loss of benefit entitlement.

The disability insurance program is financed by part of a payroll tax paid half by the covered employee and half by the employer, and a tax paid by self-employed people on their earnings. Persons who have not contributed to the Social Security system are not eligible for benefits. The disability insurance program is administered by the Social Security Administration.

The Supplemental Security Income Program

The Social Security Administration administers a second program that pays benefits to the disabled. Also part of the Social Security Act (Title XVI), the supplemental security income program (SSI) provides benefits to the nonaged blind and disabled in financial need, as well as to people aged 65 and over who are in financial need. While disability insurance provisions are a fairly recent addition to the Social Security Act, aid to the needy blind dates back to the original Act of 1935. Under the 1950 Social Security amendments, federal matching funds were also provided to states that wished to provide public assistance payments to persons who were ''permanently and totally'' disabled. In 1974, SSI, a federally administered and financed program of assistance using a federal definition of disability and a uniform federal payment standard, replaced these various federal/state programs.

SSI, unlike DI, is not a social insurance program but a welfare program. Benefits are based upon one's current income status, unrelated to past contributions or work history. The program provides a federal minimum level of income to those disabled who meet income and resource tests. As of July 1983, SSI benefits of $304.30 per month for an individual and $456.40 for a couple were the maximum amounts payable to those with virtually no other income. As income from other sources increases (excepting certain disregards), SSI payments are reduced. About 2.3 million blind or disabled persons under age sixty-five were receiving benefits under the supplemental security income program at the end of 1982.

Workers' Compensation

Workers' compensation is a system of state-sanctioned insurance programs that are to provide protection against loss of income, medical expenditures, or death due to injuries on the job. While the first workers' compensation program was enacted in the early 1900's, it was not until 1949 that all states had adopted workers' compensation programs. By 1978, nearly 90 percent of the labor force was covered by programs which would compensate for work-related accidents or occupational diseases.

Since it is a state program, workers' compensation lacks uniformity among jurisdictions in coverage, benefit structure, and administration. Unlike DI and SSI, which by definition include only the most severely disabled, workers' compensation is designed to cover the entire range of disabilities, of which only a small percentage are long-term and severe. As a consequence, workers' compensation has developed a far more flexible eligibility/benefit structure that can differentiate between permanent and temporary, as well as total and partial disability (Joe and Bogatay, 1980).

Workers' compensation is intended to protect employees from health hazards at their place of work. As a consequence, benefits are closely tied to the work-relatedness of the disability. In general, to qualify for benefits, the employee must have sustained an injury or been killed in performing his duties, but the injuries or death must not have arisen due to the employee's gross negligence, willful misconduct, or intoxication. Workers' compensation programs are financed almost entirely by employers. In 1980, the total paid under the various state and federal workers' compensation plans was about $13.3 billion.

Vocational Rehabilitation Services

The three programs just reviewed provide cash benefits to disabled workers. Their purpose is to partially replace income lost because of a disability. There exists another set of programs which provide services to the disabled, services intended to rehabilitate. The largest of these is the vocational rehabilitation (VR) program.

All beneficiaries of the DI and SSI programs are categorically eligible for consideration for state vocational rehabilitation services. By statute, all beneficiaries who have the potential to engage in substantial gainful activity must be referred for consideration. To serve these clients the states administer three vocational rehabilitation programs: a basic state program, and two special programs mandated by the Social Security Act—one for DI beneficiaries (paid out of the Social Security Trust Fund), and the other for SSI beneficiaries (paid out of general revenues). The federal government funds 100 percent of the special programs and 80 percent of the basic program.

Services of all forms can be provided to the disabled under VR programs— medical, psychological, training, tools, and placement. These services are to be provided to any severely disabled individual, without regard to financial need, under two conditions: there is a physical or mental disability that results in a substantial impediment to employment, and there is a reasonable expectation that vocational rehabilitation services may benefit that individual in terms of employment. The purpose is to rehabilitate individuals towards "maximum participation in gainful employment" (Joe and Bogatay, 1980, p. 46).

In 1977, expenditures for all three programs exceeded $1 billion and about 1.9 million received services. Of these, close to 300,000 were claimed "rehabilitated," at a cost of about $3,000 per rehabilitation (U.S. Department of Health, Education, and Welfare, 1978b).

Commonality of Programs

The common element underlying each of the programs described above is their relationship to work in society. These programs only offer benefits to a disabled person *who cannot work in the marketplace*. They either try to make that person "more employable," or give him or her a stipend. Even rehabilitation services, with their emphasis on "vocational rehabilitation," have been seen from their inception in 1920 as a way of saving money and increasing industrial output, rather than as a method of reintegrating disabled people into society (Erlanger *et al.*, 1979). Both disability insurance and workers' compensation benefits are contingent upon labor market participation, while the supplemental security income program incorporates in its disability definition the criterion of the capacity to engage in substantial gainful activity. Because women have historically had weaker ties to the labor maket, this benefit contingency on labor market participation has meant that these programs have been less responsive to the needs of disabled women.

Women and Disability

The Social Security Administration's (SSA) 1972 Survey of Disabled and Nondisabled Adults provides the best available data on the prevalence and nature of disability among adult American women. It also provides data on womens' participation rates in the disability insurance and supplemental security income programs. Two findings emerge: (1) women represent a somewhat greater proportion of persons in the population who report suffering from one or more chronic conditions or impairments, and yet (2) women are less likely than men to receive public income maintenance benefits (Allan, 1976; Posner, 1981; Krute and Burdette, 1978). The implications of these two findings for the economic well-being of the disabled woman in the United States are very serious.

Sex Differences in the Prevalence of Disability

In the 1972 SSA Survey, disability prevalence was found to be greater among women than among men (15.2 percent of women had some impairment compared to 14.0 percent of men). Not only were women more likely to report a chronic disease or impairment, but the condition was more likely to result in a severe disability. Eight percent of the women but only 6 percent of the men reported that they were severely disabled. Table 6.1 displays these different prevalence rates by sex.

The 1976 Survey of Income and Education conducted by the Bureau of the Census reports similar findings. Of the 28.2 million people three years old and older who were reported to have some activity limitation due to a health condition, about 53 percent were women (U.S. Department of Health, Education, and Welfare, 1979a).

When these differences are looked at by major disease group, women report higher rates of cardiovascular diseases (primarily peripheral vascular disorders such as varicose veins, and high blood pressure), mental disorders, urogenital conditions, neoplasms, and endocrine disorders. According to the Social Security Administration, the excess of urogenital and endocrine disease among women is due to disorders of the female reproductive system and to thyroid problems, respectively. More women than men also report visual problems—serious difficulty seeing or blindness.

While accidents and injuries caused a significant proportion of the chronic diseases and/or impairments reported by SSA survey respondents in general, on this dimension women are underrepresented. The proportion of men with an accident-related condition ranged from 16 percent of the nondisabled to 31 percent of the currently disabled. The comparable figures for women were 5 percent and 18 percent, respectively (Krute and Burdette, 1978).

Looking at other demographic variables, the composition of the disabled is heavily weighted toward older people. Most chronic conditions and impairments take years to develop. For any condition, the rates for persons aged 55 to 64 are from one and one-half to three times higher than for persons under 45. Not only are older persons more likely to suffer from a chronic condition or impairment, but also they are much more likely to be disabled

TABLE 6.1
Disability Prevalence Rate (per 1,000 population), by Sex

Population	Men	Women
With chronic conditions	464.7	507.3
Disabled	139.6	152.4
Severely disabled	59.0	85.0

Source: Aaron Krute and Mary Ellen Burdette, "1972 Survey of Disabled and Nondisabled Adults: Chronic Disease, Injury, and Work Disability." Social Security Bulletin 41:4 (1978): 10.

as a result. But as Allan points out, "Some of the relationships between age and disability may . . . reflect the work-related definition of disability. Regardless of health, many people begin to work less in their late fifties and early sixties as a mode of preparation for retirement. . . . The availability of social security benefits reinforces the effects of ill health on encouraging retirement" (Allan, 1976).

As with age and sex, the composition of the disabled population is heavily weighted toward those with low educational attainment. More than 40 percent of the severely disabled group had no high school education. As expected, blacks and other nonwhites are more heavily represented among the disabled than among the general population.

Finally the disabled population—in particular, the severely disabled—is composed of unmarried individuals to a larger extent than the nondisabled population. Since the disabled are older than nondisabled, they are more likely to be widowed, separated, or divorced.

Work Limitation and Disability among Women

Women not only report themselves as more disabled , they also report more serious work limitations as a result of their disability. In 1976, the Bureau of the Census found 13.3 percent of the 124.6 million Americans between the ages of eighteen and sixty-four reporting some level of work disability. A breakdown by sex, marital status, and household relationships as they reflect level of work disability shows some significant differences (see Table 6.2).

The implications for women of the data in Table 6.2 as regards their receipt of benefits under current U.S. programs for the disabled are important. First, the data make clear that women suffer more serious work disability than men. Their disability is more likely to prevent them from working at all, or from working regularly. The disparity between men and women on these measures is observable from age 30 onward, and steadily increases with age.

Women who suffer a work disability are also more likely than men to be living without a spouse. This sex-related difference is greatest among those women whose disability is severe enough to prevent them from working. Additionally, the extent of disability found among persons who are the head of their households is greater for women than for men. One in five women in female-headed households have some work disability; the comparable figure for male-headed households is one in eight. In the case in which the work disability is severe, female-headed households are twice as likely to have a head unable to work than are male-headed households.

Women are therefore more likely than men to be limited or prevented from working because of their disability, are likely to experience a higher degree

TABLE 6.2
Work Disability Status of Persons Aged 18–64, by Sex and Selected
Characteristics (U.S., 1976)

Characteristic	With a Work Disability (Percent of total)							
	Total		Prevented from Working		Unable to Work Regularly		Able to Work Regularly	
	M	F	M	F	M	F	M	F
Total	13.3	13.3	5.1	6.4	1.4	2.1	6.7	4.9
Age								
18–24	6.4	4.9	1.3	1.2	0.6	0.5	4.5	3.1
25–29	7.6	6.2	2.0	1.9	0.7	1.0	4.9	3.3
30–34	8.1	8.2	2.4	2.9	0.9	1.5	4.8	3.7
35–44	10.2	11.5	3.2	4.5	1.2	2.0	5.8	5.1
45–54	18.3	19.0	7.6	9.4	1.7	3.0	9.1	6.6
55–64	29.4	29.5	14.7	17.9	3.6	4.3	11.2	7.2
Marital status								
Married, spouse	13.0	11.8	4.7	5.3	1.2	2.0	7.1	4.5
Married, no spouse	11.9	17.7	3.5	8.5	1.3	3.8	7.1	5.4
Household relationship								
Head of household	13.2	20.5	4.8	9.9	1.3	3.4	7.1	7.3
Wife of head	—	11.8	—	5.4	—	2.0	—	4.5
Unrelated individual	14.2	19.3	6.1	10.3	1.9	2.5	6.1	6.5

Source: U.S. Department of Health, Education and Welfare, Office for Handicapped Individuals. *Digest of Data on Persons with Disabilities* (Washington, D.C.: Government Printing Office, 1979) Table 5, p. 17.

of work disability at an earlier age than men, and are more likely to be without a spouse. Being married is particularly important to disabled persons because the presence of a spouse provides greater income and extra attention to personal care needs. Each of these factors support the urgent need of women to have available to them some form of public income support protection. But because of womens' more tenuous ties to the labor force, and the contingent relationship between disability programs and labor force participation, women are largely excluded from public disability benefits.

Labor Force Participation of Women

At the beginning of 1983, forty-eight million American women were in the labor force—about 47 percent of the country's entire labor force, and 53 percent of all women 16 years of age and over. By contrast, 76 percent of all men aged 16 and over were in the labor force (U.S. Department of Labor, 1983). Most women who worked outside the home do so in clerical occupations (34.9 percent) and service sector jobs (17.9 percent). Of the 5.6 million women in professional and technical jobs in 1976, nearly 40 percent were elementary and secondary school teachers (U.S. Department of Labor, 1977).

While labor force participation by women has been increasing steadily in the last 30 years, women still constitute about three-fourths of the population outside of the labor force. Most of these women do not want jobs because of their home and family responsibilities. Thus women who head families (especially divorced women) are more likely to be in the labor force than wives living with their husbands.

Women's participation in and rewards from work outside the home differ from men's in several ways. First, women are more likely than men to work part-time or only part of the year. The Bureau of Labor Statistics reports that of the 46.3 million who were employed in 1977, 42.1 percent worked all year (50-52 weeks) at full-time jobs, and 33.8 percent worked at part-time jobs. The comparable percentages for men are shown in Table 6.3.

In addition to working less than full time, women have been on their current job a substantially shorter time, on average, than men. The largest differences are for persons age 45 to 64. These differences are highlighted in Table 6.4.

Thus, in 1973 the median number of years on the current job for all women employed was 2.8 years while for men it was 4.6 years.

A final dimension upon which women's relationship to work outside the home differs from that of men's is compensation. The great majority of working women have not yet attained parity with working men in earned income. Women who worked at year-round, full-time jobs in 1977 earned only 59 cents for every dollar earned by men. This figure is actually down from the 1955 level of 64 cents for every dollar. A recent Department of Labor report notes: "Men's median weekly earnings exceeded women's by $116, so that a woman had to work nearly nine days to gross the same earnings men grossed in five days" (U.S. Department of labor, 1979). The situation is no better if educational level is taken into account. In both 1970 and 1974, the median income of women college graduates aged 25 and over who worked full-time was only 60 percent of the comparable male median income (U.S. Department of Commerce, 1976). Surveys of starting salaries of women and men graduating from college have for many years revealed differences in

TABLE 6.3
Work Experience of Women and Men, 1977

Work Experience	Women	Men
Persons who worked		
Number (in thousands)	46,379	60,717
(Percent)	(100)	(100)
Worked at full-time job	31,077	53,112
50 to 52 weeks	(62.9)	(74.0)
27 to 49 weeks	(18.6)	(15.2)
1 to 26 weeks	(18.5)	(10.7)
Worked at part-time job	15,302	7,603
50 to 52 weeks	(33.8)	(32.7)
27 to 49 weeks	(25.3)	(24.4)
1 to 26 weeks	(40.9)	(42.9)

Source: U.S. Department of Labor, Bureau of Labor Statistics. *A Statistical Portrait of Women in the U.S.: 1978* (Washington, D.C.: Government Printing Office, 1980), Table 7.1, p. 55.

"offers" received by women and men job seekers. The majority of women continue to receive lower offers than men.

Thus, as most women workers continue to be concentrated in lower paying occupations that provide limited opportunities for advancement, and as discrimination in hiring, promotion, and pay scales continue to be a major obstacle to equality for women in the workplace, women's rewards from work outside the home are significantly less than men's.

Women and Public Programs

All of the factors just reviewed as regards the labor force participation of women help explain why women receive fewer and less generous benefits from pubic disability programs. Fewer women than men are in the labor force, and therefore fewer are eligible for coverage under disability insurance or worker's compensation programs. Women engaged in full-time homemaking activities do not participate in the Social Security system at all, and therefore are not eligible for DI benefits should they become disabled. To be fully insured under the disability insurance program, workers must have contributed through their payroll taxes, a prescribed number of quarters within a prescribed period of time. Both length of time worked during the year and tenure on the job, less for women than men, thus may exclude women from benefit enti-

TABLE 6.4
Median Number of Years Worked at Current Job, Women and Men by Age,
1973

Age Group	Median Number of Years	
	Women	Men
Total, 16 years and over	2.8	4.6
16 to 19	0.6	0.6
20 to 24	1.2	1.2
25 to 34	2.2	3.2
35 to 44	3.6	6.7
45 to 54	5.9	11.5
55 to 64	8.8	14.5
65 and over	10.9	13.9

Source: U.S. Department of Labor, Bureau of Labor Statistics. *U.S. Working Women: A Databook* (Washington, D.C.: Government Printing Office, 1977), Table 56, p. 57.

tlement under DI. And since DI benefit levels are indexed to earnings, even women workers covered under the program will receive substantially lower benefits than men if they become disabled. Program participation rates make clear the disadvantage disabled women face vis-à-vis our current public policies on disability.

Participation of Women in Disability Programs

In 1981, of the 46.4 million women in the labor force, 38 million were insured by the Social Security Administration in the event of disability. A quarter of these were young women, under age 25. As would be expected, coverage increases with age. About 74 percent of working women under age 25 were fully insured, 78 percent of those aged 25 to 54, and 88 percent of those 55 and over (U.S. Department of Health, Education, and Welfare, 1981). Thus, in 1981 nearly 9 million American working women were without disability insurance protection under Social Security. While there are more men in the labor force than women, fewer men were uninsured (about 3 million).

Within the Social Security program, disability insurance benefits play a smaller part in providing income replacement for women than for men. Of the 1.88 million workers who were receiving DI benefits in 1976, 1.15 were men and 730,000 were women. In the Social Security Administration 1972 Survey of Disabled and Nondisabled Adults, only 9 percent of severely disabled women were found to be receiving benefits because of their disability. Fully one-third (33 percent) of the severely disabled men were receiving benefits. Additionally, twice as many severely disabled men as women received benefits for early retirement. The situation was reversed for dependents' benefits. Twice as many severely disabled women as men received benefits as dependents of disabled, retired, or deceased workers (Allan, 1976).

For the disabled worker, benefit levels vary by sex. The average benefit received by men in 1979 was $399.40; the average benefit received by women was $281.10. Those persons more recently gaining eligibility had, on average, higher benefits awards than earlier eligibles. A woman worker who became eligible for DI benefits in 1961, for example, would be receiving an average monthly amount of $79.70. One becoming eligible in 1981 would average $320.70 (U.S. Department of Health and Human Services, Table 58, 1981). For those wives of disabled workers whose entitlement was based on children in their care, their average monthly benefit amount in 1979 was $101.60 (U.S. Department of Health and Human Services, Table 66, 1981).

The average age of women workers who are receiving disability insurance benefits is about 52 years old. Fully 67 percent of women DI beneficiaries are between the ages of 50 and 64. And it is these older disabled women workers who receive the lowest benefit levels from the program, and who are more likely to have fewer resources available to them. Many are widowed, divorced, or separated. Thus while fewer disabled women than men benefit from the disability insurance program, even those who do remain seriously economically disadvantaged.

While underrepresented in the disability insurance program, women are overrepresented under supplemental security income. Public assistance is a more important source of income for women than for men, and becomes increasingly important with the severity of the limitation. Women now constitute about 60 percent of SSI beneficiaries reflecting their weaker labor force attachment. For those women who have worked too little to gain eligibility under the disability insurance program, or who while eligible may only qualify for minimum DI benefits, public assistance in the form of supplemental security income offers the only means of support.

Public income maintenance programs such as workers' compensation and veterans disability programs are also less important for women than for men (see Table 6.5). A study done in 1975 on the workers' compensation program of five states found that 82 percent of claimants were male and only 18 percent were female (Joe and Bogatay, 1980).

Rehabilitation services are available infrequently to disabled women. Due to the VR screening process and inadequate funding, not all individuals eligible for VR services receive them. Only one-quarter of those awarded disability insurance or supplemental security income benefits in a given year are

TABLE 6.5

Receipt of Public Income Maintenance Benefits, by Severity of Limitation and Sex, 1972

(Percentage distribution of noninstitutionalized adults, aged 20–64)

Severity of Limitation and sex	Number (in mil.)	Total Percent	Receiving Public Income Maintenance					Not Receiving Publ. Inc. Maint.
			Social Security			Public Assist.	Other	
			DI	OASI	Other			
Total	104.9	100	1.4	1.4	1.8	2.3	8.3	84.9
Men	49.8	100	2.1	1.4	.4	1.3	11.9	83.0
No loss	41.0	100	.2	.8	.2	.8	11.0	87.0
Minor	3.4	100	4.0	4.7	1.0	2.8	15.6	71.9
Moderate	1.9	100	9.7	5.8	—	3.2	22.7	58.7
Severe	1.7	100	20.7	4.0	.2	4.5	16.8	53.8
Dependent	1.1	100	23.3	3.2	4.8	7.6	8.4	52.8
Women	55.2	100	.7	1.3	3.2	3.1	5.0	86.6
No loss	43.9	100	.1	.8	2.4	1.9	5.1	89.7
Minor	5.2	100	.9	2.5	4.9	4.4	4.6	82.7
Moderate	1.8	100	3.4	5.9	6.5	12.3	3.8	68.1
Severe	1.8	100	4.9	3.0	9.7	9.7	5.9	66.8
Dependent	1.5	100	11.4	4.2	9.1	11.6	6.4	57.3

Source: Iris Posner, "Functional Capacity Limitations and Disability, 1972," in *Disability Survey 72: Disabled and Nondisabled Adults,* research report no. 56 (Washington, D.C.: U.S. Department of Health and Human Services, Office of Research and Statistics).

referred for rehabilitation services. Less that half of those referred are accepted into the program. Thus eight out of every nine beneficiaries do not receive VR services (Joe and Bogatay, 1980). And those who are referred are young— 36.5 years old for DI clients, 29.8 years old for SSI clients (U.S. Department of Health, Education and Welfare, 1979b). The typical disabled woman, however, is more likely to an older recipient, and thus more likely to be screened out of the vocational rehabiliation process as having a lower potential for engaging in substantial gainful activity after rehabilitation. This bias towards providing services to individuals who can reenter the labor force often works against women who may have been full-time homemakers, or who may have had tenuous labor market connections prior to the onset of their disability, or who may now be at an age where reentry into the labor force would be difficult because of age discrimination.

Conclusions and Policy Implications

After 20 years of development, disability policy in the United States is undergoing a serious reassessment. The role and function of disability insurance, public assistance, and rehabilitation services in the life of the disabled individual, both male and female is being questioned. Application rates for the disability insurance program are rising, and so are the costs. Between 1970 and 1981, the cost of DI cash benefits grew from $3.0 to $17.2 billion. Yet the program experience for the period 1968 to 1978 reflects, in the words of one author, "disquieting trends in terms of future cost potential, an apparent erosion of the rate in which disabled beneficiaries leave the benefit rolls for reasons other than death or the attainment of retirement age" (Joe and Bogatay, 1980, p. 132). Since 1960, yearly "recoveries" have remained constant at approximately 40,000 although rolls have been steadily rising. In effect, then, over 90 percent of those who become DI beneficiaries never "recover." The resulting loss to the society of the economic contributions of these individuals is causing great concern. Countless proposals have recently been made to alter the various disabilty programs in such a way as to strengthen the incentives to renter the labor force for those disabled who can, to increase the adequacy of public benefits for those who cannot, and to make more effective and efficient the available rehabilitation services (Sussman and Hagan, 1977; U.S. Advisory Council on Social Security, 1979; U.S. Senate Finance Committee, 1979).

All of these proposals, if adopted, will strengthen U.S. policy on disability so as to more greatly benefit all disabled persons, men and women alike. But marginal improvements in program specifics will not solve what is a continuing problem for women: the strong relationship between program benefit entitlement and labor force participation. As long as the major (and most generous) disability protection programs are premised upon a model of life-long, full-time employment outside the home, with disability being explicitly defined in a work-related context, women will continue to be disadvantaged.

The policy implications of this "disadvantage" are different of course, for women who are employed and those who are not. For the majority of the 53 percent of American adult women who are now in the labor force, disability insurance benefits under Social Security provide the primary income assurance program in the event of disability. Yet only 32 percent of recent successful applicants for the DI program were women, and of those applicants who were denied benefits, more than three-fourths had incomes under $4,000. And for those women who qualify as beneficiaries, benefits remain low. Over 42 percent of female workers who are severely disabled are classified as service workers. These workers typically earn low wages (the median usual weekly earnings of full-time women service workers in 1976 was $109), and about 31 percent have less than a high school education (U.S. Department of Labor, 1977). Thus such workers would not only receive low benefits, but would be poor candidates for retraining.

The low benefits awarded women workers who become disabled result in a dramatic decline in their income. In 1970-71, 82.8 percent of recently disabled adult women experienced a drop in their yearly earnings of 50 percent or more (U.S. Department of Health, Education and Welfare, 1979a). This decline has a differential effect on disabled women with spouses and those without. The estimated median family income of severely disabled married women in 1977 was $9,543. For nonmarried women the figure was $2,225 (Lando and Krute, 1976).

Thus, if they can qualify, employed women can rely upon disability insurance benefits in the event of disability. But these benefits are likely to be very low and present a particular hardship for women who have no spouse present. Some older women who do not qualify for DI benefits on their own work record may be eligible for a disabled widow benefit under social security. But this category is very restrictive, serves few women, and provides a very low average monthly benefit.

For those 47 percent of women outside the labor force, fewer options are available in the event of disability. If married, they may qualify for the supplemental security income program. For these disabled women, their annual income guarantee would be no more than $3,652 about 84 percent of the poverty line in this country.

The implications of the above data are clear. There is need for an urgent reassessment of the impact of current disability policy on the disabled woman. While labor force participation rates of women are on the rise, social circumstances of child rearing and homemaking will always keep large numbers of women from working outside the home. Increasing divorce and separation are also enlarging the number of female-headed households in this country. The presumption that the disabled woman will either be protected from a loss of income because of adequate disability insurance protection or by the presence of a spouse is patently false. As long as those presumptions underlie major U.S. disability programs, women will remain unprotected from the economic threats associated with disability.

References

Allan, K. H. 1976. "First findings of the 1972 survey of the disabled: General characteristics." *Social Security Bulletin* 39: 10, 18-37.

Erlanger, H. S., W. Roth, A. Walker, and R. Peterson. 1979. "Disability policy: The parts and the whole." Discussion Paper. Madison, Wisc.: University of Wisconsin, Institute for Research on Poverty.

Joe, T. and A. Bogatay, eds. 1980. *The Social Security Disability Insurance and Supplemental Security Income Programs*. Washington, D.C.: The University of Chicago Center for the Study of Welfare Policy.

Krute, A. and M. E. Burdette. 1978. "1972 survey of the disabled and nondisabled adults: Chronic disease, injury, and work disability." *Social Security Bulletin* 41: 4, 3-17.

Lando, M. E. and A. Krute. 1976. "Disability Insurance: Program issues and research." *Social Security Bulletin* 39: 10, 3-17.

Posner, I. 1981. "Functional capacity limitations and disability." *Disabled and Nondisabled Adults*. SSA Report No. 56, Disability Survey 72, Chapter 4. Washington, D.C.: Social Security Administration, Office of Research and Statistics.

President's Committee on Employment of the Handicapped. 1977. *One in Eleven: Handicapped Adults in America*. Washington, D.C.: U.S. Government Printing Office.

Singer, J. W. 1978. "It isn't easy to cure the ailments of the Disability Insurance Program." *National Journal* 10: 715 719.

Sussman, M. B. and F. E. Hagan. 1977. "Worker's compensation and rehabilitation: Policy and program recommendations." Mimeographed paper.

U.S. Advisory Council on Social Security. 1979. "Social Security Financing and Benefits." Final Report. Washinton, D.C.: U.S. Advisory Council on Social Security.

U.S. Congress, Senate Finance Committee. 1979. "Issues related to Social Security Act Disability Programs." Ninety-Sixth Congress, 1st session.

U.S. Department of Commerce. 1976. *A Statistical Portrait of Women in the U. S.* Bureau of the Census. Current Population Reports. Series P-23, No. 58. Washington, D.C.: U.S. Government Printing Office.

———. 1980. *A Statistical Portrait of Women in the U.S.* Bureau of the Census, Current Population Reports. Series P-23, No. 100. Washington, D.C.: U.S. Government Printing Office.

———. 1982. *Statistical Abstract of the U.S.: 1982-83*. 103rd edition. Bureau of the Census. Washington, D.C.: U.S. Government Printing Office.

U.S. Department of Health, Education, and Welfare. 1974. *Social Security Handbook*. Washington, D.C.: U.S. Government Printing Office.

————. 1978a. *Federal Assistance for Programs Serving the Handicapped.* Office for Handicapped Individuals. Washington, D.C.: U.S. Government Printing Office.

————. 1978b. *State Vocational Rehabilitation Agency Program Data: Fiscal Year 1977.* Rehabilitation Services Administration. Washington, D.C.: U.S. Government Printing Office.

————. 1978c. *Social Security Bulletin: Annual Statistical Supplement, 1976.* Social Security Administration. Washington, D.C.: U.S. Government Printing Office.

————. 1979a. *Digest of Data on Persons with Disabilities.* Office for Handicapped Individuals. Washington, D.C.: U.S. Government Printing Office.

————. 1979b. *RSA Annual Report: 1978.* Rehabilitation Services Administration. Washington, D.C.: U.S. Government Printing Office.

————. 1980. *Social Security Bulletin: Annual Statistical Supplement, 1977-1979.* Social Security Administration. Washington, D.C.: U.S. Government Printing Office.

————. 1981. *Social Security Bulletin: Annual Statistical Supplement, 1981.* Social Security Administration. Washington, D.C.: U.S. Government Printing Office.

————. 1983. "Social Security in review." *Social Security Bulletin* 46: 1-2.

U.S. Department of Labor. 1977. *U.S. Working Women: A Databook.* Bureau of Labor Statistics. Washington, D.C.: U.S. Government Printing Office.

————. 1979. *The Earnings Gap Between Women and Men.* Women's Bureau. Washington, D.C.: U.S. Government Printing Office.

————. 1983. "Current labor statistics." *Monthly Labor Review* 106: 57-71.

U.S. Office of Management and Budget. 1979. *Special Analysis, Budget of the United States Government: Fiscal Year 1979.* Washington, D.C.: U.S. Government Printing Office.

7

Assertiveness Training for Women with Visual Impairments

Cynthia Kolb

An assertiveness support group was designed for five women with visual impairments who were attending college. The purpose of the group was to apply concepts underlying assertive behaviors (Phelps & Austin, 1975) in order to manage effectively the psycho-social factors related to adjustment to a disability (Wright, 1960; Donaldson, 1980). Issues such as developing assertive responses other than eye contact, defining a sense of personal power in handling the dependency associated with impairment, and identifying strategies for dealing with the stereotypes of others were discussed. Although no formal measurements of the group's effectiveness were made, verbal feedback from participants at the end of the five month program indicated that they felt quite positive about the experience. Further research is recommended to explore various designs and evaluations of group programs, especially to measure the impact of a disabled facilitator upon group process. Evaluating the significance of combining assertiveness concepts with psycho-social components of adjustment to a disability is also encouraged.

Background

During the past decade our society has experienced an awakening sensitivity to the meaning of civil rights for minorities. Blacks, Hispanics, and women are examples of groups that have felt the power and pride of their united energies. The handicapped, as a collective advocacy force, have only recently demonstrated a sense of community in their efforts, brought together by the bonding of shared goals and beliefs in the value of common experiences (Hull, 1979). The stigma surrounding the words "disabled" or "handicapped" is slowly being replaced by an association with potential for action and influence. Advocacy roles and creation of coalitions of persons with handicaps, the striving for consumer input, and the challenge of attaining attitudinal/architectural accessibility are responsibilities currently assumed by individuals who are physically impaired (Hull, 1979).

There has been a catch, however, in the growth of an acknowledged, cohesive power base of people with disabilities, due perhaps to the lack of a positive group identity and visible emergence of effective role models, especially for handicapped women. For blacks, black is beautiful; for women, power is sisterhood; for disabled—well, a healthy collective spirit, divorced from the maudlin images of poster children, is slow to come. But the conception of a dynamic, perceptive social movement has begun, spurred by individuals with disabilities merging their newly found autonomy with the knowledge and skills to bring social change. Their integrity arises from insisting upon the right to define individual life satisfaction. Having spokespeople who can draw strength and resourcefulness from their experiences of being disabled, who have the verbal ability to address issues, pinpoint methods of resolving problems, and employ their handicaps as a way to highlight messages for affirmative action are key to the maintenance of a productive civil rights movement.

The idea of women with physical limitations taking responsibility for themselves and implementing change, however, is fairly recent. Our culture has told us that the disabled as a group are to be pitied, avoided, or condemned (Goffman, 1974). Disability has implied not only a difference in mobility and functioning but also in character. A physical restriction becomes the focal point for judging an individual's personality, academic/vocational possibilities, social-sexual potential, and life happiness (English, 1971).

Because of our country's investment in physical independence and ability as a life-style, a handicap is frequently perceived as a threat to the nondisabled because it represents a situation that could happen to anyone, at any time, and is a phenomenon to be avoided. We constantly receive many messages about how important physical mobility and attractiveness are. Advertisements tell us to look and live like Princess Di, yet telethons sell the "helplessness" of a handicapping condition, and the disabled were previously isolated at home or socially avoided. The fear of dependency, realistically or not associated with a disability, has pervaded our culture's understanding of women who are handicapped. The humanness of women with physical limitations, therefore, has not been seen; their handicaps defined their worth. Our society's fear and lack of awareness about the commonality of the human experience maintained these stereotypes. Such assumptions encourage women with handicaps to be categorized and kept at a social distance. Apprehension about persons who have physical differences are not dealt with, but sustained.

A handicapped woman, therefore, not only has to handle her own feelings in adjusting to a disability but also must mange the attitudes of others. A handicap may bring forth judgments about one's personal worth and social acceptability, not unlike assumptions made about women in general because of their sex. Women have been characterized as needing protection and desiring dependency, with their main source of identity coming from being mothers or spouses. A female's attractiveness has been defined in terms of a mate's approval and her ability to raise a family. Again, the person's intrinsic skills, values, and expected behavior are overshadowed by external qualities.

What do these cultural norms mean for a woman who is disabled? Her strength as an individual in taking responsibility for herself, being able to interact with others and deal with the demands of daily living, may be disregarded. Any imagined or real physical dependency often negates her status as a prospective partner or capable employee. Perhaps, most importantly, a handicapped woman faces a struggle in defining her self-esteem and social-sexual identity. She has been told that a woman should resemble the body beautiful image idolized by our society, that "making it" means living up to the expectations for perfection we so desperately pursue. Looking different indicates not that she is an individual, but that she is inferior. Instead of learning to value herself and her body according to her personal standards of worth, she may focus on how she varies from the norm and so miss the beauty of her uniqueness.

Dealing with the above external pressures throughout one's life requires a fairly healthy self-concept, positive body image, and freedom to take risks (Wright, 1960). Yet how does a woman with an impairment acquire such qualities when cultural pressures frequently have focused on her limitations so that approval from others becomes more important than her personal affirmation?

Program Rationale

Assertiveness training appears to offer a basis for building interpersonal skills and learning how to reinforce a healthy self-esteem (Phelps & Austin, 1975). Morgan and Leung (1980) conducted an assertiveness training program with physically disabled college students and found that subjects who participated in the sessions demonstrated improvements in inventories that measured acceptance of disability, self-concept/esteem and social interactions. Mishel (1978) also stated that handicapped persons who completed assertive training reported increased assertive behaviors in their life experiences. Such behavioral skills can enhance a disabled individual's effectiveness in interpersonal and self-advocacy situations (McFall & Marston, 1970).

There is a lack of discussion in the literature, however, about the design of assertiveness sessions for disabled women. Attention has not been focused on the psycho-social factors that may be related to disability and subsequently affect the refinement of assertive behaviors. How does a woman with a visual impairment, for example, compensate for an inability to establish eye contact as she assertively handles a situation? What does help mean to a handicapped woman and how can she manage necessary assistance so that her personal power and independence are enhanced? Can she create strategies in a self-affirming manner for dealing with assumptions that may be made about her because of her disability? Can she channel her anger in being stereotyped by others into actions that enrich her self-esteem and range of choices for inner satisfaction?

The Present Program

An assertiveness support group for women with visual impairments was formed at Wayne State University to explore the above issues. Women volunteered for the program that initially was to run for 11 weeks but lasted for five months. All group members had visual impairments and came from varied backgrounds: one woman was single and in the third year of law school while the second was divorced with two children and studying social work. The third and fourth members were married and undecided about their majors; the fifth woman was a senior in English. Two women had had visual impairments since childhood and the remaining group participants had lost their sight when they were either adolescents or young adults.

The purpose of the group, which met on a weekly basis for one and a half hours, was to discuss the principles of assertive behaviors, explore women's communication patterns, and develop strategies for effectively managing a disability. A counselor, who is a handicapped woman, facilitated the group and combined the behavioral principles of assertiveness training (Phelps & Austin, 1975) within an experiential group framework (Lakin, 1972). An experiential orientation stresses the communication between members as a valuable vehicle for self-understanding and greater interpersonal effectiveness. Leadership within the group is shared and participants are encouraged to initiate interactions.

During early sessions, the facilitator directed discussions about components of assertive behavior, with an emphasis on relevant concepts (Phelps & Austin, 1975; Jakubowski, 1977). As women became familiar with assertive principles, such discussions became less frequent. Members, however, were consistently encouraged to relate the group's communication dynamics to assertiveness constructs. The facilitator shared experiences in living with her disability upon request from other members or when she considered such self-disclosure appropriate. It is important to note here that there has been no research about the impact of a disabled facilitator upon group process. Such investigation is becoming increasingly essential as more handicapped professionals enter the counseling field.

As stated previously, early sessions were spent defining the differences between assertive, aggressive, and passive behavior, (Phelps & Austin, 1975) along with identifying what members had been taught from family, friends, and our society about their roles as women and as disabled individuals. Ways of expressing assertive behavior, such as voice, facial expression, body posture, gestures, and eye contact were also specified. Since most women were not able to see others' expressions, attending to cues such as their physical position in relation to another person and quality of voice were additional methods of displaying assertive responses.

The importance of physical contact for a visually impaired woman in communicating assertively was emphatically shown in one session where several women were very concerned about a member's lack of trust in others. While a few women leaned towards her as she spoke, the untrusting woman was unable to see the caring in the body movements or faces of people near her. At that moment, it seemed essential for group members to establish physical contact with each other so that they could nonverbally experience trust and caring. A volunteer, therefore, was asked to lie on the floor while the other members lined up on either side of her and, in unison, slowly lifted her from the ground. Women were instructed to rock her back and forth gently, and to be aware of the group's movement as a whole. After a few minutes, the woman being held was gradually lowered back to the floor. Trust shown through a shared, caring effort that was experienced physically and emotionally quickly helped the group move to a warmth that was apparent. Women seemed to be freer in reaching out—in hugging or emphasizing a point by touching, by seeing through their fingers, hands, arms. Using physical personal space became a useful component of assertive behavior.

Along with discussing the qualities comprising assertive interactions, roles that members perceived themselves assuming because of their sex and physical condition were also clarified. Some felt that the presence of a handicap negated their rights to express anger or stand up for their beliefs. Others questioned the "shoulds" and "should nots" of saying "no," compromising too much in relationships or playing down their social needs. Learning how messages from others complemented or contradicted their personal beliefs was helpful in defining individual self-perceptions and values. A disability would not as a result mean that a woman is helpless, a burden, overly sweet, or bitter. A woman could learn to appreciate herself, feel positive about her power and use it effectively. Women realized that they weren't alone in their uncertainties or fears: knowing that their needs or desires were not abnormal encouraged members to build confidence in their judgment and potential for change.

The basic tenets of an assertive philosophy outlined by Jakubowski-Spector (1974) and "Everywoman's Bill of Rights" (Bloom, 1978) were useful guides in pursuing the meaning of another aspect of assertive communication classified as personal needs and rights. One individual, for example, talked about the overprotectiveness experienced from her family after her sudden sight loss. Independence became important to her as she acquired mobility skills, started college and lived in an apartment. Her need was for autonomy; her right was self-sufficiency. Yet her family struggled to anticipate solutions for future problems she might encounter and thus maintain her dependence on them. Discussing her home experience brought forth feelings about her sight condition, especially in terms of handling physical dependence along with her emotional independence. Needing assistance did not imply that she was essentially incapable, required protection, or had to be cared for. The student, however, had to work through feeling inadequate because she sometimes relied on others for help. The awareness that necessary assistance allowed her to be more independent and that she could have a great deal of control over her life by arranging for needed aid gave some breadth to her concept of personal power. Support from other women who shared the belief that accepting help can be part of an individual's lifestyle was also invaluable. We all need, we all receive, and we all give help.

Help, though, is a double-edged interchange. It is usually much easier to give than receive over time. Women frequently talked about the frustration they experienced in having to explain their needs repeatedly. Dealing with the attitudes of those who were insensitive or prejudged them because the women relied on aid from others was a strain in certain situations, even for women who were positive about themselves. Women initially learned from one another that it was helpful to discuss their aggravation or anger about negative reactions from those around them and that such perceptions need not determine how they perceived themselves.

Personal vulnerability was most apparent for members in understanding the process of how they handled reactions from others. An articulate member brought out an incident where she felt uneasy about using a cane which would allow her greater mobility in traveling on a city bus. The stigma attached to a white cane was difficult for her to handle, and her identity was threatened by an external symbol of blindness. Since she was partially sighted, the student was unsure about whether people would see her as not really needing a cane and taking advantage of a system, or else entirely helpless. Refining how she felt about herself became a primary tool for developing the inner resource-fulness needed to deal with negative reactions and her own uncertainties. The abilities she had, support from family and friends which reaffirmed her value, and the ways she rewarded herself, were intrinsic assets she could use in handling interactions. The attitudes of others many times could not be con-trolled or changed. The best resource available to her was the awareness that her disability was only one part of her, not the whole. She was not solely defined by others' assessments of what she should be, based on what she could or could not do, but rather by who she is and would like to be. And with assertiveness, that meant believing in one's right to have emotions, needs, fears—to try and not only succeed, but also fail—to trust one's assessment of a situation and attempt new behavior.

What women valued about themselves and others reflected the vitalness of establishing positive support systems, both from within the members themselves and from significant persons in their lives. The group itself grew into a supportive environment where women practiced listening more effectively, using "I" statements, and role playing different ways of dealing with situations. As the group cohesiveness stabilized, the women seemed invested in understanding how they interacted with each other, so that assertive principles of expressing one's beliefs while being aware of others could be incorporated in each session.

At the end of five months, members seemed to have an understanding of their values in communicating and integrating assertiveness as part of their behavior. A few women emerged as strong models who had learned how to maintain their self-respect and deal with anxieties in living by acting, rather than refraining from involvement. All members verbally experienced an improved sense of mastery over their lives and greater self-satisfaction.

The idea that women need not settle for second best in intimate relationships, careers, or friendships came through clearly. The possibilities, therefore, of asking a man out for lunch or initiating other dating activities was not only theory, but also practice! Instead of using energy to repress their feelings, women began to tap their strength for living. An individual could subsequently build a bridge from personal life satisfaction to a concerted advocacy role. And with that bridge new leadership for a social movement by the disabled can emerge, with handicapped women assuming key power positions.

Recommendations/Summary

As members of two minority groups, disabled women contend with double stereotypes that often set limiting parameters for them in defining a meaningful quality of life. Combining assertiveness training with strategies for managing a disability may provide handicapped women with effective living skills. Much more research is needed both in terms of the content of an assertiveness training program and measurements of a group's impact on participants. The resources and talents represented by disabled women can no longer be ignored, their viability no longer denied. The sense of personal power possible through assertive behaviors, plus the self-affirmation available through a support group, suggest that group programs offer a constructive approach for disabled women to embrace as they advocate for the right to life satisfaction and opportunity.

References

Bloom, L.Z., Coburn, K. & Perlman, J. 1978. *The New Assertive Woman.* New York: Dell.

Donaldson, J. 1980. "Changing attitudes towards handicapped persons: a review and analysis of the literature." *Exceptional Children* 4(7): 504-14.

English, R.W. 1971. "Correlates of stigma towards physically disabled persons." *Rehabilitation Research and Practice Review* 2(4): 1-17.

Goffman, E. 1974. *Stigma: Notes on the Management of a Spoiled Identity.* New York: Jason.

Hull, K. 1979. *The Rights of Physically Handicapped People.* New York: Avon.

Jakubowski, P.A. 1977. "Assertive behavior and clinical problems of women." In Rawlings, E.I. & Carter, D.K. *Psychotherapy for Women: Treatment for Equality.* Springfield, Illinois: Charles C. Thomas.

Lakin, M. 1972. *Interpersonal Encounter: Theory and Practice in Sensitivity Training.* New York: McGraw-Hill.

Mishel, M. 1978. "Assertion training with handicapped persons." *Journal of Counseling Psychology* 25(3): 238-41.

Morgan, B. & Leung, P. 1980. "Effects of assertion training on acceptance of disability by physically disabled university students." *Journal of Counseling Psychology* 27(2): 209-12.

McFall, R.M. & Marston, A.R. 1970. "An experimental investigation of behavior rehearsal in assertiveness training." *Journal of Abnormal Psychology* 76: 295-303.

Phelps, S. & Austin, N. 1975. *The Assertive Woman.* California: Impact.

Wright, B. 1960. *Disability: A Psychological Approach.* New York: Harper & Row.

8

A Peer Counseling Training Program for Disabled Women: A Tool for Social and Individual Change

Marsha Saxton

This article presents a description of a successful peer counseling training program for disabled women, offered in a community-based self-help organization. The program provides both training in peer counseling skills and a personal growth experience. It was carried out in a group context specifically designed for the needs of women with disabilities. The counseling approach, the training format and curriculum, and the evaluation procedures can all serve as a basis for agencies interested in developing similar programs.

Introduction

The women's movement of the 1960s and 1970s taught us the potential of group activities by and for women. Women's groups have provided a strong counterforce to oppression and have led to the empowerment of the individual. The success of the book, *Our Bodies, Ourselves* (Boston Women's Health Book Collective, 1972), gives testimony to the power of self-help for women.

Disabled women, like their able-bodied sisters, can benefit greatly from peer groups. Being female and disabled in our culture often means experiencing the overlap of two kinds of oppression. Together they often lead to a double measure of isolation and powerlessness. A disabled woman in a peer group can realize she is not alone in her feelings about her unique body and uncommon life circumstances. She can meet and learn from others who have confronted similar experiences, and she can look forward to change. A peer counseling training group can be a particularly powerful forum for this process. By building on their own experiences in such a group, participants

95

acquire and share valuable counseling skills for use in assisting each other's growth.

Thus, the purpose of the group is dual: to train participants in the use of counseling skills and to provide a therapeutic group experience. This paper presents a model of a peer counseling training program for women with disabilities offered in a community-based self-help organization called the Boston Self Help Center.

Disabled Women

The concerns of disabled women are unique and deserve special consideration. The cultural interactions between sexism and the oppression of disabled persons (or "able-bodiedism") serve to reinforce each other in the personality of the individual. For example, sexism in this culture perpetuates traits of passivity, dependence, and childishness in women. These traits dissuade women from excelling. Able-bodiedism produces the same effects and similarly results in a reduced likelihood of success. The cultural standards of physical attractiveness exacerbate this situation. Women in this culture are beset with messages from the media to buy products to alter aspects of their appearance which do not conform to established standards of beauty. Disabled people similarly are made to feel that they must hide their bodies. Disabled women who do not conform to cultural standards of beauty are doubly stigmatized.

Thus, the issue of sexuality can often present difficulties for disabled women. The problems stem from two sources: those problems which are a result of actual physical limitations, and those which are a result of myths and attitudes. Many of the cultural assumptions regarding sexuality are particularly hurtful to disabled people. The include such social "rules" as: Sex should not be discussed or planned, but should be "spontaneous," and sexual intercourse and orgasm are necessary for sexual satisfaction.

These assumptions may lead to a sense of failure for women with physical limitations requiring adaptations, special planning, or assistance. These social myths interfere with the realization that sexuality is not limited to specified "acts" or set behaviors. When these beliefs are recognized as myths by the individuals, the problems arising from physical limitations seem much less formidable.

Myths regarding disabled persons include the common assumption that disabled persons are asexual, either because they are incapable of sexual function or because they just "shouldn't want it." Some sexual preferences, such as homosexuality, are often considered to be particularly bizarre among disabled persons.

Because of sexism, women's skills and intelligence are minimized. In the area of sexuality, women may perceive a chance to redeem themselves as highly valued. Disabled women, however, because of the myths and assumptions regarding sexuality and disability, are not offered this chance at redemption, and therefore may be made to feel particularly worthless. It was interesting to note that some disabled women, self-identified as "feminists," have felt a conflict between the goals of feminism and their personal needs. The feminist movement encourages women to resist being regarded as sexual objects and targets of objectifying sexual comments from men, while many disabled women have never been such targets and wish to "have a turn" at being viewed as a sexual or "sexy" person.

The disabled individual faces many psychological adjustments. Unfortunately, this is often made considerably more difficult by the social and attitudinal barriers which the disabled person is likely to encounter among family, friends, and others.

The disabled person may face the gamut of behaviors from the able-bodied world ranging from gawking to avoidance, from pity to resentment, or from vastly lowered expectations to awe. Along with these attitudes, disabled persons confront a variety of tangible barriers: architectural inaccessibility, lack of interpreter services for deaf persons, and lack of Brailled or taped materials for blind persons. In addition, disabled persons, particularly females, confront less tangible barriers: discrimination in employment, second-class education, and restricted opportunities for full participation in the political life of the community. Consequently, the disabled woman may often experience feelings of self-hate, hopelessness, isolation, unworthiness, or ugliness.

Peer Counseling

A peer counselor is in a unique position to assist another disabled person in dealing with life issues. Peer counseling is a process by which one person is helped by another person who has had similar or related experiences. The concept and practice of peer counseling is gaining increased attention. Professionals in a variety of helping fields are beginning to recognize and utilize this effective resource. Egan, in *The Skilled Helper*, notes:

> There is a growing body of opinions and evidence . . . that helpers with extensive training in psychological theory and a variety of academic credentials do not necessarily help, and that the para-professional helper, if properly trained in helping skills, can become very effective even without extensive training in psychological theory (1975: 9).

Peer counseling has gained special significance in the field of rehabilitation. Title VII of Public Law 95-602 (the 1978 Rehabilitation Amendments) provides statutory authority for the use of peer conselors in Independent Living Centers. The purpose of these centers is to train severely disabled persons in attaining the maximum degree of independence needed to live in a community-based setting. The new mandate is in large part a result of a growing disability rights movement demanding greater consumer involvement in the provision of human services.

The practice of peer counseling can address many of the issues facing disabled persons involved in the rehabilitation process. A useful definition is offered by Schatzlein:

> Peer counseling is a necessary adjunct to the rehabilitation process, in which a severely disabled person who has made a successful transition from institutional to independent community living, provides resource information, support, understanding and direction to another disabled person who desires to make a similar transition (1978: 4).

Frequently, the peer counselor will offer training in adapting to the physical demands of a disability. For example, the peer counselor may assist a peer client with wheelchair mobility or wheelchair maintenance. The peer counselor may also share knowledge and experience in coping with the broader aspects of disability, such as obtaining social security benefits from governmental agencies or locating accessible housing and transportation.

The peer counselor can also be instrumental in helping an individual confront various emotional aspects of disability. The approach described here emphasized the psycho-social aspects of disability. The assumption is that an individual's ability to function in the psycho-social sphere often shapes his or her ability to cope with the various aspects of dealing with a disability. This may include one's ability to perform medical and nonmedical self-care, revise vocational goals, and negotiate reactions of family and friends to one's disability.

A Model Program

The following is a description of the peer counseling training program for disabled women held at the Boston Self Help Center (BSHC). The purpose of the group was to provide training in peer counseling skills as well as a personal growth eperience.

The theoretical basis for this peer counseling program was derived primarily from the works of Robert Carkhuff (1977). Simply stated, the counselor facilitates an atmosphere of trust and genuine respect wherein the client can express feelings without fear of judgment on the part of the counselor. It is assumed that clear thinking and decisive action will result after the client has had the opportunity to ventilate openly fears, anger, grief, and other emotions. It is also assumed that maximum growth occurs when responsibility for life decisions are made by the client him/herself. Thus, the counselor rarely offers advice or gives interpretation.

This particular counseling approach views the individual as the target of numerous emotional social hurts. These hurts begin at an early age and serve to create self-limiting behavior patterns. The individual can recover from these distresses, and regain a more rational grasp of his or her life, if given the necessary emotional support and resources.

One significant aspect of this approach is the concept of oppression, here defined as "the systematic invalidation of one social group by another." Participants are encouraged to examine the effects of oppression (not only sexism and able-bodiedism, but other types such as racism and classisms) on their own personalities. In group discussions, participants identify cultural myths and stereotypes, focusing on those aimed at them personally. Participants realize that the cultural messages are often so strong that individuals accept them as true and thereby perpetuate the myths. The reversal of this "internalized oppression" is a major goal of the training.

The nature and limitations of the peer counseling relationship are clearly defined in the training. Basically, the peer counselor is expected to meet regularly with the client to provide a setting where the client may discuss ideas, express feelings, set goals and report back on them. The peer counselor is *not* expected to solve the client's problems, socialize with the client, or attempt to meet the client's personal needs.

Peer counselors are trained to determine the difference between life issues which are manageable in the peer counseling context, and those which are not. If they are not, the client is referred to an appropriate professional.

The peer counseling training group was run by a leader and an assistant leader, both disabled women, who are staff counselors at the Boston Self Help Center. The group leader (this author) developed the training program and the assistant leader was trained as a peer counselor and group leader in this program.

The training group was planned for an initial 12 week period, with continuation for additional time negotiable with leaders and participants. At the time of this writing the group is in its eighteenth week.

The group was advertised in the BSHC's schedule-of-events mailing. Prospective participants were interviewed by one of the group leaders. The interview assessed the applicant's ability to:

- Acquire and utilize the counseling theory and techniques.
- Form relationships.
- Communicate caring with other group members.

- Follow through in attending group sessions and practicums.
- Actively utilize peer counseling skills in some capacity following the completion of the group.

Four of the participants' group fees were funded by a grant from the Massachusetts Rehabilitation Commission. The others were charged on a sliding scale basis depending on income.

The training group was cross-disability in composition, which afforded participants' exposure to a wide variety of disability types, yet with focus on the commonalities of life experiences. This is consistent with BSHC's philosophy that alliance with differing interest groups will result in effective social change for all.

The group was composed of eight women, including two leaders, and ranged in age from 25 to 42 years. All were disabled (including the following disabilities: cerebral palsy, arthritis, post polio, spina bifida, visual impairment, upper-extremity amputation), were white, and of lower middle to middle class. Five participants were employed, either part or full time, one in college and two unemployed. Four members had had some type of emotional counseling or therapy prior to this group.

The group leaders, by functioning as participants, helped create an atmosphere of trust and ''peerness,'' enabled the leaders to model the role of ''active client,'' and encouraged openness and risk-taking in sharing of feelings.

Evaluation questionnaires were administered to participants following 12 weeks of group meetings, asking for evaluation of the group on the following dimensions:

- Effectiveness of leaders' teaching skills.
- Impact of the group on personal growth, independent living skills and vocational readiness.
- Effectiveness of the counseling approach, particularly as related to being female and being disabled.

Training Curriculum

The training format of the two hour weekly training sessions typically included:

- Lecture and discussion on weekly topics.
- Demonstrations of counseling techniques before the group.
- Short practice sessions.
- Feedback and discussion about the practicum counseling sessions.
- Personal sharing by group participants.

The practicum counseling sessions held between pairs of group members were scheduled outside of group time. These served to reinforce skills learned, and allowed each individual to take a turn as "counselor" and as "client." A portion of every training group session was devoted to supervision of the practicum counseling sessions.

The following is a description of the curriculum for the first 12 weeks of the group:

Session 1 was devoted to the introduction of members and explanations of basic theory used in the peer counseling program. Participants were given the opportunity to explore and identify areas of their own lives they wanted to focus on in the practicum sessions.

Sessions 2 and 3 focused on counseling techniques, including active listening, role-playing, and the use of fantasy.

Session 4 explored the use of self-appreciation validation of others and means of exposing and contradicting feelings of inadequacy. The need for warm, open expression of respect, affection and appreciation of the peer client in individual sessions as well as in the training group was stressed.

Session 5 emphasized aspects of body image and loss, as they relate to disability and chronic disease. Here, discussion focused on societal standards of acceptable appearance and the influence of the "Youth and Beauty" cultural orientation on self-image of disabled women. Counseling techniques eliciting self-appreciation and body awareness were presented.

Session 6 explored the nature of cultural oppression of disabled persons, including aspects of discrimination, stereotypes, etc. Emphasis was placed on identifying ways disabled persons internalize these cultural messages and the use of counseling techniques to contradict this.

Sessions 7 and 8 focused on the impact of sexism on women in general and on disabled women in particular. Counseling techniques were demonstrated to expose and contradict internalized feelings of passivity, powerlessness, unworthiness, etc. The interaction of the effects of sexism and the oppression of disabled persons was discussed.

Session 9 focused on Independent Living. Goal setting and problem solving techniques were presented as ways to overcome barriers to maximal self-reliance for disabled women. Community resources were reviewed here.

Sessions 10 and 11 focused on sexuality and sexual relationships. Here sexuality was linked to issues previously discussed, including sexism and stereotypes regarding disability. Participants were encouraged to share how early childhood training as well as experiences in relationships influenced sexual self-image.

Session 12 focused on overcoming feelings of isolation in male and female relationships. Participants set goals to overcome barriers in achieving full personal and social lives.

Participants' Reactions

The peer counseling skills gained in this program provided each individual with a sense of effectively assisting others in areas where she herself had experienced difficulties. She could now draw upon her experiences as a means of offering support. This sense of being able to assist others is extremely important for severely disabled persons, because it opposes the cultural notion that people with disabilities have little to offer. Several individuals noted that the tone of the group, that of "moving toward social change," helped participants feel that they were learning valuable skills for use in the disability rights movement, and not just "making people feel better." One group member stated:

> I feel that my abilities as a counselor have grown with each session. The opportunity to observe and participate in counseling sessions in the group, getting feedback from other members and leaders, has been valuable. The weekly "co-counseling" sessions with one person are invaluable. Being a member of this group has given me more confidence in myself and in my ability to interact on different levels and thus participate more fully in the disabled rights movement. I have worthwhile ideas and thoughts to contribute.

With the increasing use of peer counseling in rehabilitation nationwide, the training allows participants to develop a marketable skill. Two of the women reported that they have taken on new counseling roles in their work places. Another is now working at BSHC as a peer counselor doing intake interviews and two others are planning to join the BSHC staff as peer counselors in the near future. Group participants who become staff peer counselors are thus realizing the goal of self-help. Many individuals who have undergone the training now work in other agencies and are training other peer counselors. Individuals often use the peer counseling training to explore an interest in counseling as a profession before undertaking schooling in that field.

A unique and important aspect of the training program at BSHC is that all peer conselors who work at BSHC are themselves members of a support group. This is an integral part of the ongoing training and supervision. It is consistent with the BSHC philosophy that effective counselors require continuing support for themselves and their feelings related to work as a counselor.

With respect to personal gains, one of the most prevalent reactions to the group was the individual realization that "I'm not alone in my experiences and feelings." Both the group sessions and the individual peer counseling sessions provided a contradiction to the feelings of isolation that often accompany being disabled. For example, one participant noted: "I have been made more aware that there are others who face many of the same issues and frustrations that I grapple with. This has lessened my feelings of separateness from the mainstream.''

The concept of cultural oppression of both women and disabled persons proved to be a valuable tool for personal growth. Participants reported experiencing a challenge to the feelings of powerlessness and a reversal of their guilt for their "failure to be normal." One participant reported:

> I see more clearly now how some of the problems I have socially, developmentally, etc., are not unique to me and are actually rooted in the systematic oppression that accompanies a disability. The phrase, "It's not your fault," as it relates to oppression is helping to allay very strong guilt patterns.

Participants revealed a greater acceptance of themselves and disabled women. One stated simply, "I feel much more proud and self-accepting. Much more." Another said:

> I've begun to see that it's [my disability] not the end of the world. With the group's help, I've begun the healing process and have begun to grow strong with self-respect and self-assurance.

Other members shared:

> The group let me explore and examine life's hurts, past and present. With the group's help, I've begun the healing process and have begun to grow strong with self-respect and self-assurance.

> My self-image and feelings of inadequacy about being a woman have been changed to the point where I have a more positive feeling about myself as a woman and as a person. Being able to share some long pent-up feelings and getting support helped.

In Conclusion

This model is by no means restricted in application to disabled women. The reciprocal client-counselor paradigm, as well as the "challenging oppression" focus, can successfully be applied to many persons of various backgrounds.

Significant components of the program that contributed to its success included:

1. Effective screening of applicants to help insure maximum benefit from the program.
2. A workable counseling approach, easily acquired and utilized by beginners, with room for expansion of skills by experienced peer counselors.

3. A training curriculum relevant to the needs of the participants which embodied both personal growth and social change.
4. Strong peer leadership by persons willing to model both the client and counselor roles.
5. An immediate channel for peer counselors' energies emphasizing on-going supervision and support.

In summary, peer counseling training seemed beneficial for disabled women in the following ways: The approach described here was able to provide a valuable and marketable skill, effectively build the confidence and self-image of participants, contradict patterns of isolation and powerlessness, and allow individuals to successfully set and attain personal goals. Peer counseling can assist individuals in attaining their optimal levels of independence, meeting vocational goals, and developing a positive self-concept. By helping individuals to recognize their full human and legal rights and by challenging culturally oppressive behaviors and attitudes which prevent the realization of their full human potential, this program thus becomes an effective vehicle for furthering the goals of the disability rights movement.

References

Arkridge, R., B. Means, T. Milligan and R. Farley. 1978. *Interpersonal Skills Training: Basic Helping Skills for Rehabilitation Workers*. Arkansas Rehabilitation Research and Training Center: University of Arkansas, Arkansas Rehabilitation Services.

Boston Women's Health Book Collective. 1972. *Our Bodies, Ourselves*. New York: Simon and Schuster.

Carkhuff, R. R. and B. G. Berensen. 1977. *Beyond Counseling and Therapy*. New York: Holt-Rinehart-Winston.

Corn, R. 1977. *Aiding Adjustment to Physical Limitation: A Handbook for Peer Counselors*. Columbia, Maryland: Howard Community College Press.

Egan, G. 1975. *The Skilled Helper: A Model for Systematic Helping and Interpersonal Relating*. Monterey, Calif.: Brooks/Cole.

Griffin, E. L. and W. Martin. 1979. "Peer counseling: Process and goal." *1979 National Spinal Cord Injury Foundation Conventional Journal*, 31st Annual Convention, August 5-9, 1979. Denver, Colorado.

Jackins, H. 1970. *Fundamentals of Co-Counseling Manual*. Seattle, Wash.: Rational Island Publishers.

Schatzlein, J. E. 1978. "Spinal cord injury and peer counseling/peer education." Unpublished paper, presented at the Regional Spinal Cord Injury Center, Dept. of Physical Medicine and Rehabilitation, University of Minnesota Hospitals.

Tracy, G. S. and Z. Gussow. 1976. "Self-help groups: a grassroots response to a need for services." *Journal of Applied Behavioral Science* 12: 381-96.

9

Women and Chronic Renal Failure: Some Neglected Issues

Nancy G. Kutner and Heather L. Gray

It has been assumed until recently that chronic renal failure is more prevalent among men than among women, but data now indicate that at least half of all renal patients are women. The literature continues to focus on adjustment problems of male patients, especially sexual adjustment and job-loss problems, and to assume that women can adjust more easily because of their ability to maintain the homemaker role. However, women patients whose work status is that of homemaker are found to have the highest depression scores, and job loss results in low satisfaction for those who have held meaningful outside jobs. Women patients are not necessarily more satisfied with their sexual life than are men patients. Questions can also be raised about women patients' access to treatment alternatives associated with optimal patient outcomes.

Introduction

More than 58,000 persons in the United States had experienced chronic renal failure (also known as end-stage renal disease or "ESRD") and were receiving some form of dialysis therapy as of 1982. Without maintenance dialysis or a successful kidney transplant, patients whose kidneys have failed would die.

Adjustment to renal failure and to dialysis therapy is inherently stressful for patients; frequently noted reactions include anxiety, depression, and loss of self-esteem (Reichsman and Levy, 1972; Abram, 1974; Anger, 1975). Although the dialysis process restores a more normal fluid and electrolyte balance and raised patients' hematocrit, many dialysis patients continue to complain of fatigue. Fatigue, dialysis treatment schedules, and employers' reluctance to hire renal patients contribute to a lowered employment rate among patients who have gone on dialysis (Kutner et al., 1980). Marked reduction in interest in sex and an inability to perform sexually are common among dialysis patients (Levy, 1978a).

Although recent data indicate that half of the persons in the U.S. who have experienced renal failure are women, existing literature on kidney patients tends to focus on adjustment problems of male patients and to assume that women adjust better or more easily than men (Czaczkes and De-Nour, 1978: 149). Moreover, there is little recognition of structural arrangements in the provision of dialysis therapy which tend to benefit men more than women.

Literature Review

Financial coverage of dialysis treatments was assumed by Medicare in September 1972.[1] Before 1972, when there were few dialysis machines available and the cost of treatment was almost $40,000/year per patient, there was a careful selection of ESRD patients who were to receive dialysis through an artificial kidney machine. These patients were typically young and had few medical complications in addition to their kidney failure.

It appears that dialysis patients prior to 1972 were also typically male. Evans et al. (1981) report that in 1967 male patients on hemodialysis (the dominant type of dialysis therapy) outnumbered female patients three to one. Data collected in 1978 in a national sample survey, however, indicated that the dialysis patient population was divided almost equally between males (49.2 percent) and females (50.8 percent). Similarly, our own survey in January 1980 of the nine centers in the Atlanta SMSA, which provide maintenance dialysis therapy to chronic renal failure patients, indicated that 500 patients were being treated; 245 of these patients were male and 255 were female.[2] It seems reasonable to conclude with Evans et al. (1981: 489) that since the passage of the Medicare legislation, women have had greater access to dialysis.

In the few studies that have focused on women as well as men renal patients, there is the suggestion that women are less likely than men to experience a significant change in social role as a consequence of renal failure. It is assumed that women's "typical" social role is that of homemaker and that women can more easily continue to fill this role despite their chronic illness than men can continue to fill their stereotypical role (i.e., paid employment outside the home).

Of 25 patients studied by Goldberg et al. (1972) following initiation of dialysis therapy, only 7 were classified as "productive" (i.e., working) and 6 of these 7 patients were women. While only 1 of the 10 male patients (10 percent) remained gainfully employed, 6 of the 15 women patients (40 percent) remained active as homemakers. (However, none of the women were employed outside the home.) Similarly, Reichsman and Levy (1972), who studied

25 patients dialyzing during 1964-1968, found that 10 of the 18 men (56 percent) were active 0-25 percent of their "available time," while 6 of the 7 women (86 percent) were active 75-100 percent of their "available time." Activity in the latter study included paid employment, housework, or school enrollment, and "available time" was defined as time which could be used for these pursuits, excluding time spent dialyzing or being hospitalized.

A more recent study (Burns and Johnson, 1976) of 102 renal patients reported a decline in employment among men patients from 70 percent to 13 percent and a decline in employment among women patients from 38 percent to 0 percent. The researchers indicated that women patients in the latter category then tended to become homemakers.

It may be an oversimplification to assume that women have fewer problems than men when adjusting to renal disease because women can continue to be homemakers or can more easily shift from outside employment to homemaking activities. Many homemaking chores are more physically demanding than an outside job, and energy level tends to be significantly lowered for renal patients. Homemaking chores may offer less sense of accomplishment to a woman than holding an outside job, if only because of the financial reward which accompanies the latter. Rosenfield (1980: 37), comparing depression scores for nondisabled men and women, reports that "when the wife is not working—when the division of labor is traditional—women have much higher levels of depressive symptoms than men."

Male patients may experience lowered self-esteem when kidney disease interferes with the patient's fulfilling the status of main income-earner for the family or contributes to sexual impotence. Levy (1978: 330) points out that these two outcomes may frequently be related for men, increasing the probability of sexual dysfunction over and above that which can be expected from the physical and endocrinologic changes associated with renal disease:

> In a household in which the male is unable to work and therefore home most of the day, with the woman of the house often assuming some financial responsibility by working, the male patient often participates more in household activity. Among men whose masculine identity is tenuous, such role reversal may produce sexual dysfunction.

Although Levy (1973) found in a survey that women dialysis patients had become less interested in sexual relations and were less likely to experience orgasm, he did not posit a concomitant decreased sense of femininity among women. It appears that the issue of sexual dysfunction among women renal patients is generally assigned less importance than is the issue of sexual dysfunction among male patients.

Although they suggested that women can adjust more easily than men to life on dialysis, Reichsman and Levy (1972:861) reported that women patients were more likely than men to express feelings of anxiety about who would care for their children if they should die. This is the only reference we have found in the literature to a source of emotional distress which is more problematic for women than for men who have end-stage renal disease. As we have noted, decline in employment and decreased sexual response are reported as characteristic of women patients who are on dialysis, but these are not viewed as problems for women while they are viewed as problems for men.

Method

Source of Data

Research on the interrelation of medical, psychosocial, and vocational characteristics of chronic renal failure patients was initated at Emory University's Center for Rehabilitation Medicine in 1978. Between January 1978 and June 1980, 150 patients were evaluated by means of written psychological tests and a semi-structured interview as well as assessment of physical strength and cognitive-motor skills. The large majority (91 percent) of these patients were undergoing maintenance dialysis therapy (primarily hemodialysis) at the time of their evaluation; the remainder had received a transplant.

Patients were identified through their use of nine dialysis facilities in the Atlanta metropolitan area and through their affiliation with a local chapter of an organization for kidney patients.[3] The resulting study population closely approximates the existing race and sex composition of the Atlanta in-center dialysis population as well as the percentage of patients dialyzing at each facility.

Nature of Sample

This article focuses primarily on data obtained from 23 white women and 27 black women who were on maintenance dialysis therapy due to chronic renal failure. Median age of the white women was 34, with a range of 18 to 67; they had been on dialysis for an average of 27.4 months. Median age of the black women was 47, with a range of 26 to 70; these women had been dialyzing for an average of 24.3 months. This age difference stems from a difference in etiology of renal disease for the two races. The most frequently recorded diagnosis for black patients was hypertension. Because white patients were more likely to have developed renal disease due to congenital abnormalities or childhood infections, their renal failure tended to occur earlier in life.

Only 6 black women in our sample (22 percent) were currently married; 14 of the white women (61 percent) were currently married. The average years of schooling which black women had completed was 10 or 11; the white women, on the average, were high school graduates who had also completed some college training.

Five of the white women, but none of the black women, were dialyzing in their own homes rather than in a dialysis facility. Data from a recent national survey of dialysis patients indicate that non-whites are significantly less likely than whites to dialyze at home (Evans, 1979a). Home patients tend to be married (and hence to have a partner available to help with dialysis) and to be more highly educated than are facility dialysis patients, both of which help to explain the lower incidence of home dialysis among black patients.

For purposes of comparison, we will also present selected data obtained in the same study from 46 white men and 40 black men who were on maintenance dialysis therapy. Median age of white men was 43, with a range of 19 to 79; median age of black men was 47, with a range of 21 to 63. White men had been dialyzing for an average of 36.5 months; black men had been dialyzing for an average of 38.0 months. Black men (55 percent) were almost as likely as white men (61 percent) to be currently married. As was true for women patients, the average years of schooling completed by black men was 10 or 11; white men, on the average, were high school graduates who had also completed some college training.

Measures

Data reported in this article were gathered from a semi-structured interview with the patient which lasted 30 to 90 minutes, from a self-rated satisfaction scale completed by the patient, and from responses to the Zung self-rated depression scale (Zung, 1965) and the Zung anxiety scale (Zung, 1971).

In addition to demographic information, patients were asked during the interview to indicate the usual number of hours spent in homemaking activities and to rate how they felt upon arising, at mid-day and upon retiring (a measure of fatigue level).

A self-rating scale was used to assess patients' satisfaction with their current working or homemaking situation, their feelings about themselves, and their current sexual life as compared to their satisfaction with these areas when they were well. Patients were asked to mark a point on a 100-millimeter line to describe their feelings, with 100 indicating "the same or more satisfying" and 0 indicating "not at all satisfying."

Both the self-rated depression scale and the self-rated anxiety scale developed by Zung consist of 20 Likert-type items. According to Zung (1965), an index score below 50 on the self-rated depression scale is within the normal range; from 50 to 56 indicates borderline depression, and a score greater than 56 indcates significant clinical depression. For the self-rated anxiety scale, an index below 44 is within the normal range; from 45 to 55 indicates significant anxiety symptoms, and a score greater than 55 indicates severe anxiety symptomatology (Zung, 1971).

Results

Patients' Employment/Homemaking Status, Satisfaction and Depression

After beginning maintenance dialysis, the modal pattern among black women in our sample was to give up employment outside the home and devote their energy to homemaking. White women were more likely than black women to continue their pre-dialysis job or student status (Table 9.1). This finding seems to be a function of socioeconomic differences between the two groups of women. The greater frequency of white women maintaining a job outside the home was linked to their ability to continue clerical or teaching positions, while black women found it difficult to continue maid work and other jobs which required them to be on their feet for long periods of time. Employers of white-collar workers may also be more understanding about dialysis patients' need for flexible scheduling of work hours or occasional absenteeism due to health problems.

Black women and white women also differed in their satisfaction with their current job or homemaking situation relative to when they were well. Among women who had given up outside employment and turned to homemaking, the average satisfaction rating was 83.4 for black women, while the average satisfaction rating for white women was 31.8. Thus, women's reaction to a shift from employment to homemaking seems related to the nature of the job

TABLE 9.1
Women Patients' Activity Status After Beginning Maintenance Dialysis

	Black Women		White Women	
	N	%	N	%
No significant level of activity	3	(11)	3	(13)
Decreased level of homemaking	4	(15)	4	(17)
Shift from employment to homemaking	10	(37)	4	(17)
Pre-dialysis level of homemaking	7	(26)	6	(26)
Pre-dialysis (or better) job or student status	3	(11)	6	(26)
Totals	27	(100)	23	(99)

held when they were employed. Black women, who had primarily held un-skilled jobs, found homemaking a more satisfying alternative than did the white women in our sample.

Women who had been able to maintain or improve their pre-dialysis job or student status were highly satisfied with their current situation. The average satisfaction rating for white women in this category was 69.3; for black women, the average satisfaction rating was 78.0. It is interesting to note the job status of the black women in this category. One had moved from a CETA position to being a full-time college student, one continued her 10 year job at the hospital where she dialyzed, and one obtained a clerical position after a vocational rehabilitation referral stemming from her participation in the research project.

Average depression scores, as measured by the Zung scale, give another perspective on patients' adjustment following initiation of dialysis therapy (Table 9.2). Among both women and men, depression scores were lower for employed persons than for individuals whose main activity was homemaking. For white women and white men, depression scores for the employed group were significantly lower than those of the homemaking group ($p < .01$). However, the only category for which significant clinical depression was evident was white men whose main activity was homemaking.

Women who said they tired easily during an average day tended to report fewer hours per week of homemaking activity; this was not a significant correlation, however.

Patients' Satisfaction with Their Sexual Life

Patients were asked to rate their satisfaction with their current sexual life compared to their satisfaction when they were well. Although decreased

TABLE 9.2
Mean Depression Scores of Renal Patients, by Race, Sex, and Activity Status*

	Black Patients	(N)	White Patients	(N)
Women whose main activity was homemaking	51.26	(19)	49.36	(11)
Employed women	50.33	(3)	39.17	(6)
Men whose main activity was homemaking	48.40	(9)	59.38	(8)
Employed men	45.57	(14)	45.48	(21)

*This table does not include patients who had no significant level of activity.

interest in sex and decreased ability to perform sexually are not the only factors likely to affect satisfaction with sexual life, patients indicated during their interviews that these factors did strongly affect their satisfaction in this area.

Average sexual satisfaction ratings of black women and white women are compared with the average ratings given by men of similar race and marital status in Table 9.3. In two comparisons, women's average satisfaction was higher than the average satisfaction reported by men. In one of the two remaining comparisons, however, men reported higher satisfaction with their current sexual life than did women, and average satisfaction ratings for men and women were quite similar in the remaining case. No statistically significant differences were found between the means shown in Table 9.3.

Thus, our data do not indicate that men patients are less satisfied than women patients with their sexual life. The large majority of patients reported decreased satisfaction with their sexual life compared to their satisfaction when they were well, and two of the mean ratings reported in Table 9.3 indicated that patients viewed their sexual life as "much less satisfying."

Patients' Anxiety

Reichsman and Levy (1972) reported that women's concern over the fate of their children if they should die created anxiety for women dialysis patients. However, responsibility for dependent children did not appear to be related to anxiety scores among women in our sample. As measured by the Zung (1971) scale, women with the highest anxiety in our study were black women with children in the home. The average anxiety score for that group, 45.50, indicates the presence of anxiety symptoms. However, this score was not significantly greater than the average score for black women who did not have dependent children at home (43.93). The latter score falls within the normal range specified by Zung (1971).

TABLE 9.3
Mean Sexual Life Satisfaction Ratings of Renal Patients, by Race, Marital Status, and Sex

| | Black Patients | | | | White Patients | | | |
| | Married | | Nonmarried | | Married | | Nonmarried | |
		(N)		(N)		(N)		(N)
Women	39.00	(4)	61.20	(15)	69.85	(13)	53.40	(5)
Men	53.67	(21)	48.60	(15)	25.44	(27)	57.60	(15)

Regardless of whether or not they had dependent children, white women's anxiety scores were well within the normal range (39.41 for those without dependent children and 32.67 for those who did have dependent children). Thus, black women generally appeared to be more anxious, as well as more depressed, than white women in our sample. Although black men did not appear to be more depressed than white men, the average anxiety score for black men (46.57) indicated the presence of anxiety symptoms and was higher than the average anxiety score for white men (43.84).

Discussion and Conclusion

In an earlier study of disabled individuals (Kutner and Kutner, 1979), we reported that the inability to perform a job was the most salient loss for all subjects. Regardless of race and sex, inability to work was regarded as the worst thing about being sick. In addition to the financial and self-esteem rewards which individuals gain from a job, renal patients in this study noted that a job has the additional benefits of giving you something to think about other than your own problems and of making you tired so that you can sleep better at night despite your physical discomforts.

In literature dealing specifically with renal patients, there is often the suggestion that women fare better than men after developing ESRD because they can carry on with their housework and still feel that they are fulfilling a significant societal role as homemakers. The data reported here raise questions about the validity of this suggestion. Women dialysis patients who held rewarding jobs outside the home prior to the onset of their disability indicated a low level of satisfaction with their current homemaking role. As Nathanson (1980) notes, employment can be an important source of self-esteem for women, buffering the individual against stresses in her environment. Although black women who had formerly worked outside the home were satisfied with the homemaking role as compared to their previous job status, these women had relatively high depression scores. For white women, continuation of job or student activities after beginning dialysis was related both to high satisfaction with current status and low depression scores. Finally, homemaking chores may be difficult for women whose illness causes them to tire easily during the day. Fatigue is a frequent complaint of renal patients.

Comments offered by subjects during the semi-structured interview indicate additional difficulties associated with the homemaker role. One women stressed the need to have something to think about besides your own problems; she was especially grateful for her job because it kept her mind off herself during the day. Two women observed that it is difficult for a wife/mother/homemaker who has renal disease when so many people depend on her and continue to expect her to fulfill their needs. Her disability is not a visible one, and therefore she may not be viewed as really sick, especially by her children. As Zahn (1973) noted, there is a tendency for interpersonal relations to be impaired when the disabled role is not clearly legitimized.

Our data suggest that women renal patients are not more satisfied with their sexual life than are men renal patients. Women patients, despite decreased sexual response, can still function as sexual partners, whereas male patients' sexual disability (impotence) is clearly defined. Research on sexual problems of renal patients has been concerned only with males (Levy, 1978b). Again, women's impairment is invisible and hence not a legitimized source of concern.

Safilios-Rothschild (1977: 4) points out that "adding to the problems of being female and disabled is often a third factor, such as age or poverty or illiteracy." The third factor which stands out in this study is minority status (i.e., being black) which, for women in our sample, in turn implies a disadvantaged socioeconomic position and a decreased probability of being currently married. These two characteristics decrease the likelihood of dialyzing at home, which is the treatment setting associated with the best patient outcomes (Evans, 1979a). We suspect also that black women are less likely to be candidates for a kidney transplant; transplant recipients in our study to date include eight white men, seven white women, four black men, and three black women.

It appears that women have only had equal access to dialysis therapy since the ESRD program was assumed by Medicare in 1972. They now have a chance to survive which they apparently did not have before 1970. However, inequities persist in addition to the homemaker and sexual adjustment stereotypes about female renal failure patients which have been questioned in this article. Structural characteristics in the provision of dialysis therapy—especially home dialysis incentives, typical sex of dialysis staff and nephrologists, and Social Security benefits—seem to benefit men more than women patients.

There is growing interest in the use of dialysis within the home as a replacement for dialysis within hospital or clinic facilities (Atcherson and Roy, 1980; Roberts et al., 1980; Evans, 1979b). The annual cost of home dialysis is significantly less than that of in-center dialysis, and increased use of home dialysis would therefore save the federal government a great deal of money. Home dialysis requires a willing partner/helper, however, who can take the time to participate in home training with the patient and will be available four to six hours three times a week to assist with the procedure. It is not surprising, then, that home patients tend to be men whose wives (or mothers) can serve as the partner. And if the home patient is a woman, the expectation that the patient on home dialysis should be the one primarily responsible for directing his/her dialysis may create an uncomfortable reversal in the traditional dominant/subordinate husband/wife roles within the family. Perhaps barriers to use of home dialysis by women patients, as well as men patients, would be significantly decreased by Medicare coverage for a trained helper or technician to go into the home; this alternative is only available on a limited, experimental basis at the present time.

Dialysis staff (nurses, social workers, dieticians) are primarily female. Male patients in our sample referred to female staff as "the girls," and it was clear that men enjoyed the attention they received from these female care-givers, who checked their blood pressure during dialysis, chatted with them, and generally administered to their needs. Nephrologists, on the other hand, are primarily male, and some women patients commented on their nephrologists' failure to be sympathetic to menstrual cycle problems brought on or increased by dialysis therapy (Levy, 1978b).

Finally, women dialysis patients may be denied access to Social Security income. Women who discontinue jobs in order to raise a family are ineligible for Social Security if they have not worked for five of the last 10 years. This problem is not specific to ESRD patients, but is one frequently noted by dialysis social workers.

The literature dealing with renal patients conveys the impression that ESRD is largely a male disease. If at least half of the patients who are currently on maintenance dialysis in the U.S. are women, further research on the issues raised in this article is clearly needed.

Notes

1. Medicare also supports the cost of kidney transplantation, but the number of patients who receive transplants is quite small in comparison to the number who are on maintenance disalysis therapy.
2. These nine facilities treat relatively stable, chronic patients. Dialysis units within two hospitals in the metropolitan area also provide treatment to acutely ill patients; these patients are transferred to another facility when they are stabilized.
3. This organization is the National Association of Patients on Hemodialysis and Transplantation (NAPHT).

References

Abram, H. S. 1974. "Psychiatric reflections on adaptation to repetitive dialysis." *Kidney International* 6: 67-72.

Anger, D. 1975. "The psychologic stress of chronic renal failure and long-term hemodialysis." *Nursing Clinics of North America* 10: 449-60.

Atcherson, E. and C. Roy. 1980. "From center to home dialysis." *Dialysis and Transplantation* 9: 489-90.

Burns, S. and H. K. Johnson. 1976. "Rehabilitation potential of a dialysis vs. a transplant population." *Dialysis and Transplantation* 5: 54-56.

Czaczkes, J. W. and A. K. De-Nour. 1968. *Chronic Hemodialysis as a Way of Life.* New York: Brunner/Mazel.

Evans, R. W. 1979a. "The Treatment of Kidney Disease: An Analysis of Medical Care Process, Medical Care Structure and Patient Outcome." Unpublished Dissertation, Duke University, Durham, N. C.

————. 1979b. "Center or home dialysis?" *New England Journal of Medicine* 301: 1186.

————, C. R. Blagg and F. A. Bryan. 1981. "Implications for health care policy: A social and demographic profile of hemodialysis patients in the United States." *Journal of the American Medical Association* 245: 486-91.

Goldberg, R. T., A. W. Bigwood, and W. Donaldson. 1972. "Vocational adjustment, interests, work values, and career plans of patients awaiting renal transplantation." *Scandanavian Journal of Rehabilitation Medicine* 4: 170-74.

Gutman, R. A., W. W. Stead, and R. R. Robinson. 1981. "Physical activity and employment status of patients on maintenance dialysis." *New England Journal of Medicine* 304: 309-13.

Kutner, N. G., H. Baker, P. Bretches, H. Chyatte, P. Fair, H. Gray, and C. Wortham. 1980. "Programs and treatments: Views of dialysis and transplant patients." *Dialysis and Transplantation* 9: 1138, 1140-42.

———— and M. H. Kutner. 1979. "Race and sex as variables affecting reactions to disability." *Archives of Physical Medicine and Rehabilitation* 60: 62-66.

Levy, N. B. 1973. "Sexual adjustment to maintenance hemodialysis and renal transplantation: National survey by questionnaire." *Transactions of the American Society for Artificial Internal Organs* 19: 138-43.

————. 1978a. "Psychological sequelae to hemodialysis." *Psychosomatics* 19: 329-31.

————. 1978b. "Sexual function in hemodialysis patients." In A. Comfort, ed. *Sexual Consequences of Disability.* Philadelphia: George F. Stickley.

Nathanson, C. A. 1980. "Social roles and health status among women: The significance of employment." *Social Science and Medicine* 14: 463-71.

Reichsman, F. and N. B. Levy. 1972. "Problems in adaptation to maintenance hemodialysis: A four-year study of 25 patients." *Archives of Internal Medicine* 130: 859-65.

Roberts, S. D., D. R. Maxwell, and T. L. Gross. 1980. "Cost- effective care of end-stage renal disease: A billion dollar question." *Annals of Internal Medicine* 92: 243-48.

Rosenfield, S. 1980. "Sex differences in depression: Do women always have higher rates?" *Journal of Health and Social Behavior* 21: 33-42.

Safilios-Rothschild, C. 1977. "Discrimination against disabled women." *International Rehabilitation Review* 1: 4.

Zahn, M. A. 1973. "Incapacity, impotence and visible impairment: Their effects upon interpersonal relations." *Journal of Health and Social Behavior* 14: 115-23.

Zung, W. W. K. 1965. "A self-rating depression scale." *Archives of General Psychiatry* 12: 63-70.

————. 1971. "A rating instrument for anxiety disorders." *Psychosomatics* 12: 371-79.

10

Toward a Model of Factors Influencing the Hiring of Women with a History of Breast Cancer

Nancy McCharen and Jo Anne L. Earp

Whether surgical treatment for cancer which results in the removal of an external part of the body is viewed by employers as a medical disability that interferes with the performance of job-related functions, or fits a more stereotypic definition of a physical handicap that might even prevent an employee from being hired, has not been adequately studied. To identify factors which influence employers' decisions to hire women who have had breast cancer, a model of factors influencing the decision to hire was developed. A random sample of personnel directors from an industrialized North Carolina county was surveyed. A majority had personal experience with breast cancer patients and had had mastectomy employees leave work. Five factors were found to explain 69% of the variance in hiring practices: size of company, level of sick leave benefits, company involvement in employees' medical insurance, employers' education, and personal experience with breast cancer. Knowledge level about the disease did not *predict the hiring decision. Regardless of whether medical personnel made the final decision, the influence of* nonmedical *factors was found to be quite strong in determining whether a former breast patient was actually hired.*

Introduction[1]

Only a very few studies have been conducted on employer hiring practices for persons with cancer or other chronic disease conditions *from the perspective of* the employer, rather than from that of the patient or job applicant. Instead, patients' perceptions of the effect of their illness on employment opportunities—either anticipated or experienced—have usually been relied upon (Craig *et al.*, 1974; Schottenfeld and Robbins, 1970).

117

The dual foci of the study reported here were to: (1) describe the employment situation for women with a history of breast cancer, and (2) test selected aspects of a conceptual model of factors thought to influence employers either to hire or not to hire women with a history of breast cancer. A review of the available literature directly bearing on the subject of employment of women with breast cancer, as well as of more tangentially related research on employer attitudes and practices toward employees generally considered handicapped or disabled, gave rise to the theoretical model shown in Figure 10.1. The specific factors in the model tested in the empirical research reported on here were the relationships among: company factors (#4), company policies (#5), the employer (#6), and actual hiring (#9). (See Figure 10.1.)

Background

Medical condition, when it is considered in the hiring process, operates most often as a negative factor, a reason not to hire someone. Initially, employers are influenced by cultural images of, and attitudes toward, particular illnesses. Jenkins and Zyzanski (1968) found in an urban Florida county that most people associate cancer with helplessness and perceive it as stigmatizing. Wakefield (1970), in numerous studies on attitudes toward cancer, notes a persistence of beliefs about its incurability and gruesome mortality. He found that nurses had an exaggerated pessimism towards cancer patients, based on their personal experience rather than on their professional training.

Legislation reflects general societal attitudes as well. While specialized legislation, such as vocational rehabilitation or affirmative action programs, may affect positively the ultimate decision to hire a woman with a history of breast cancer, it can also result in labeling. This, in turn, may contribute to the formation of social stigmas that restrict those people to certain kinds of jobs or set quotas on the number of such people able to be hired.

Categorical legislation, while providing protection to former cancer patients, may also result in labeling and social stigma for those protected. The Vocational Rehabilitation Act of 1973 pertaining to the handicapped can be interpreted as including former cancer patients (Tokarski et al., 1976). Both New York (1973) and California (1975) include former cancer patients in state labor codes prohibiting employment discrimination. To date, any stigmatizing impact as well as assessment of the benefits of such legislation has not been reported in the literature.

Attitudes related to factors *within* business organizations have also been shown to serve as deterrents to hiring individuals with particular medical histories. McKenna (1974) finds that employers in these situations fear that the employee may need great amounts of sick leave, may cause an increase in health insurance for all employees, and may cause workmen's compensation

FIGURE 10.1
Theoretical Model of Factors Influencing the Hiring of Women with a History of Breast Cancer

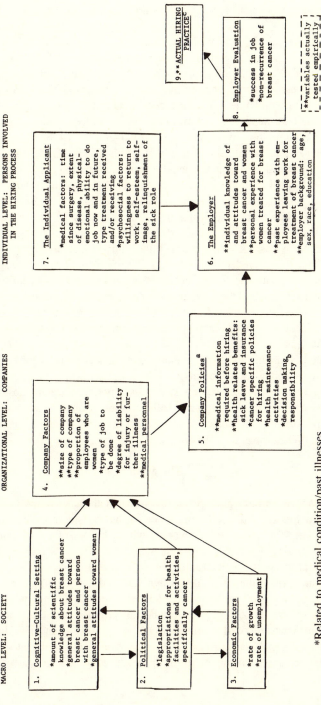

*Related to medical condition/past illnesses.

**Whether the final decision maker is medical or nonmedical.

***Reported past practice: whether or not a company has ever hired a woman with a history of breast cancer.

to increase. McKenna, however, does not test the validity of these suppositions.

In a survey of 125 industrial physicians, Weinstock and Haft (1974) found that although willingness to hire a person with chronic ailments varied with the type of illness and job application, factors such as company liability for further illness, possible increase in cost of compensation insurance and possible loss in work time also influenced the decision to hire. They conclude that "The criteria used for determining employability appear, in some cases, to have little relation to modern medical judgement" (p. 83).

Organizations debate the utility of a preplacement physical examination versus a medical history questionnaire completed by the applicant (Williamson, 1971; Voelz and Spiekard, 1975). But few question the requirement that medical information is necessary for hiring. Contrary to the beliefs of many employers, however, at least one researcher has shown that preemployment medical ratings are poor predictors of later job performances, at least in nonhazardous positions. In a double blind study of a medically nonrestrictive hiring policy, Alexander et al. (1975, 1977) found, at one year, no significant differences on number of days out of work for sickness or in quality of work performance between those labeled "no medical risks" regardless of actual condition and those labeled as "risks" on the basis of actual medical conditions. They concluded that preplacement employment physicals are not cost beneficial.

Indeed Feldman (1978) notes that former cancer patients took *fewer* sick leave days and worked harder than other employees, probably to combat employer and co-worker expectations of poor performance and absenteeism. A study done by the Metropolitan Life Insurance Company suggests that the work performance of cancer patients is no different from that of other employees (Wheatley et al., 1974).

The Model

The above findings gave rise to the theoretical model proposed in Figure 10.1. Factors external to the job applicant but considered influential in affecting employer practices for women with a history of breast cancer were identified on three levels: macro (society), organizational (companies), and individual (persons involved in the hiring process).

On the basis of the model it was hypothesized that the employer, building on his/her own personal knowledge and experience and influenced, in addition, by societal factors shaping attitudes toward disease and disability, takes into consideration specific company policies as well as an individual applicant's condition *before* arriving at an evaluation of the applicant's potential. The applicant is then either hired or not hired based on that employer's

evaluation. On the basis of cost considerations and other practical considerations, only four parts of the model were actually tested in the research reported
on here: company factors (#4), company policies (#5), the employer (#6),
and actual hiring practice (#9). The latter concept served as the dependent
variable in this research; it was operationalized as "reported past employment
practices regarding the hiring of women known to have a history of breast
cancer."

Methodology and Study Design

Though primarily a descriptive study using a cross-sectional design, provisions were made to tentatively test associations among a number of variables
included in the model. The survey took place in 1977 in an industrial county
in central North Carolina. Fifty-seven percent of the women age 16 and over
in the county in that year were in the labor force. For women age 45 to 64
(i.e., those most likely to develop breast cancer), 63 percent were in the labor
force. Hence, it was assumed that many, if not most, large companies had
been exposed to women employees with a history of breast cancer, either
those already on the job or those seeking a new position.

The population for the survey was all employers in the county. The term
"employers" was used in this research to refer to those persons responsible
for hiring job applicants. Thus, the unit of observation was an individual
rather than a company. Respondents were mostly experienced, college-pre-
pared, white, middle-aged, upper and middle level management personnel,
79 percent of whom were male.

Two sampling frames, one industrial (125 companies) and one non-indus-
trial (73 establishments), were used to obtain a random sample of all places
of business in the county. The only exclusions from the sample were those
establishments whose work force numbered fewer than 25 employees or whose
employee population was totally male.

A 50 percent sample from each frame was randomly selected. Eleven places
had to be eliminated, some no longer in business, others because they did
not meet the size or sex-specific criteria used for inclusion in this study.
Eighty-seven self-administered anonymous questionnaires were distributed to
the individual in each company responsible for making the final hiring decisions; 68 were returned for a 78 percent response rate.

The procedure used to deliver the questionnaires included several steps:
(1) to assure us that the respondents did, in fact, meet the definition of
employer, and (2) to obtain as high a response rate as possible. Introductory
letters to each company were followed up by telephone calls to confirm that
the company met the requirements for inclusion in the study and that the
individual receiving the letter satisfied the definition of employer. The re-

searchers then visited each company to answer general questions the participants might have about the study and to leave the questionnaire along with a stamped envelope. A week after the visit, follow-up letters were sent to all participants.

The 68 returned questionnaires represented 34 percent of the combined sampling frames. However, the final sample size for analyses involving the dependent variable question "To your knowledge, has your company ever hired a new employee with a history of breast cancer?" was smaller than 68 because of the "don't know" responses (the responses were: 29 percent "no"; 25 percent "yes"; 46 percent "don't know"). Because questionnaires were anonymous, it was impossible to follow-up the "don't know" responses in order to classify them as either "yes" or "no." Thus, we took the conservative position and discarded them, reducing the sample size to 37 for analyses involving that variable. Although the study was an exploratory one, multivariate analytical techniques were used despite the small sample size; relationships that emerged from such procedures, we reasoned, would have to be very strong in order to reach statistical significance.

As indicated earlier, correlations between hiring practice and selected variables in three of the eight different categories of the model were examined. Of the 19 variables originally hypothesized to be related to hiring practice, several were dropped before analysis (e.g., explicit cancer policy and race of decision-maker) because of insufficient variation in their distributions. Others were not included in the series of multiple stepwise regressions subsequently performed because they were not significantly related ($p<.05$) to hiring practice in bi-variate analyses. Of the remaining 13 independent variables, a two-stage series of stepwise regressions with hiring practice revealed eight to be strong predictors of past practice. These 8 were then tested in a final regression model.

Results

Corresponding to the two major objectives set forth at the beginning of this article, the results are divided into two sections. In the first section the employment situation, including characteristics of the companies, company policies, and characteristics of the employer-respondents themselves, is described; all variables initially expected to influence the decision to hire or not to hire women with a history of breast cancer are defined. In the second part of this section, an analysis of the relationships between the dependent variables and selected independent and interviewing variables is presented in an attempt to assess more specifically the utility and validity of particular components of the theoretical model shown in Figure 10.1.

Characteristics of the companies (Factor 4)

More than two thirds of the 68 companies participating in the study were manufacturing plants; the remainder were businesses engaged in performing services, or in trade, transportation, finance, or government work. Businesses ranged in employee size from 25 to 5,000, with 170 the median number of employees per establishment. About 60% of the companies had a majority female workforce. Fewer than half had their own, on-site medical personnel company doctors or occupational nurses.

Company Policies Relating to Breast Cancer (Factor 5)

Fifty-five percent of the companies surveyed required medical histories of applicants before employment. Of these, 70 percent required preemployment physicals.

Sick Leave

The majority of respondents reported that sick leave benefits were affected most by length of service. Thirty-four percent said that type of job affected sick leave benefits while only 13 percent reported that type of illness affected such benefits.

In 44 percent of the cases, the minimum qualification for sick leave was either no days or fewer than five days. In contrast, in more than one-third of the cases for those considered "minimally" qualified, more than 11 sick leave days were allowed. For employees with the maximum qualification for paid sick leave, only one-third of the companies allowed either no days or five or fewer days. Over half the respondents reported that for employees with the maximum qualifications for sick leave, 11 or more days annually were allowed. Clearly, the definitions of "minimum" and "maximum" sick leave, as well as of "qualified" employee, varied widely in this sample. This variation foreshadowed the importance of the sick leave factor in the multivariate analysis used to test the conceptual model of hiring practices.

Medical Insurance for Employees

In only 6 percent of the cases was the company totally uninvolved in employees' medical insurance (to cover hospital and doctor charges) for those working full time. By contrast, 40 percent reported that the company paid the entire premium and all employees were covered. Fifty-four percent said that the company paid part of the premium for all (or some) employees and employees paid the other part.

Only three people said that their insurance prevented them from hiring individuals with particular medical histories (specifically heart, lung, and skin diseases, or tuberculosis).

Health Maintenance Activities

Thirty-six percent of the companies surveyed reported that they provided preventive health or screening activities for their employees, often on company time (71 percent "always," 24 percent "sometimes"). Eleven companies had provided breast cancer education one or more times.

Almost half (46 percent) of the respondents said that they considered health education for employees and staff an appropriate function of companies such as theirs. Twenty-six percent did not think it an appropriate function and 28 percent were not sure.

Responsibility for Hiring

The final decision to hire women with a history of breast cancer was seldom made by a medical practitioner (15 percent). Most often, the personnel director made the decision (42 percent). The future supervisor (26 percent) and other company personnel such as a vice president (17 percent) were others cited as responsible for the final decision.

Regardless of who was the final decision maker, 81% of the respondents consulted with other person(s) before making such a decision. In 25 percent of the cases, this other person was the applicant's personal physician.

Cancer Policies

Though no company at the time of the survey had an explicit cancer policy, some respondents did know of other companies having such policies. Seven percent knew of companies requiring prospective applicants to be five years symptom-free of cancer before they would hire them. Thirteen percent said they did prefer, although did not require, persons with a history of malignancy to be symptom-free for five years.

The Employer (Factor 6)

The respondents themselves were persons holding middle or upper level positions (14 percent company presidents, vice-presidents, or agency directors; 24 percent personnel directors; 19 percent other administrative/managerial; 18 percent personnel managers) with a substantial amount of work experience. Their median number of years in personnel work was 10, with a median of 5 years in their current position as the person with a major responsibility for hiring.

They were a well-educated group, 62 percent having a college degree (BA, BS) or higher; 84 percent had family incomes over $16,000 annually (1977). The median age of respondents was 39. All were white and 79 percent were male.

Experience with Breast Cancer

Many respondents had experience with women with breast cancer both at work and among friends and family members. Three-fourths knew someone personally who had had breast cancer, and almost half had had employees leave work for treatment of this disease. Of the 27 respondents who had employees leave work for this reason, 48 percent reported that the women were absent from work on the average fewer than 8 weeks. Thirty-seven percent reported the usual absence of employees for treatment of breast cancer was between 8 and 13 weeks. One-quarter of the respondents said that their companies had hired new employees with a history of breast cancer; 29 percent said that their companies had not; and 46 percent did not know if they had.

Knowledge About Breast Cancer

Many of the respondents had incomplete knowledge about breast cancer. While 88 percent knew, correctly, that contact with someone who has cancer cannot cause the disease, 75 percent thought, incorrectly, that a blow to the breast could cause breast cancer. Only half of the respondents knew that women aged 45 to 60 were those most likely to develop breast cancer.

Testing the Theoretical Model

The 13 variables which together comprised the three major components examined in this research (company factors, company policies, and employee attributes) were first correlated separately with actual hiring practice (Table 10.1). These correlations suggested that items from each of the three major independent variable categories would, when combined, yield the strongest explanation of hiring practice.

Trying a number of stepwise regression models using different combinations of the factors shown in Table 10.1 yielded a group of eight variables, five of them significant at the $p < .05$ level. All eight factors, along with their beta values, are shown in Table 10.2. The principal factors predicting whether or not a company had ever hired women with a history of breast cancer are: size of company, level of sick leave benefits, company involvement in the payment of medical insurance premiums, employer's education, and personal experience with women with a history of breast cancer. These factors together explain 69 percent of the variance in company hiring practices. The employers' level of knowledge about breast cancer, as well as their sex and age, plus the percentage of the company that is female, when looked at in combination with other variables, have little impact on hiring practices (Table 10.2).

TABLE 10.1
Coefficients for Selected Variables with Hiring Practice

Variable	Coefficient	p value	Implied Relationship
Type company	.32	.028	Non-industrial—have not hired Industrial—have hired
Size company	.52	.001	≤ 225 employees—have not hired > 225 employees—have hired
Percent of employees who are women	−.23	.085	Less than 50%—have hired More than 50%—have not hired
Company medical personnel	.38	.011	No medical personnel—have not hired Have medical personnel—have hired
Sick leave	−.48	.002	Low sick leave—have hired High sick leave—have not hired
Insurance	.11	.254	——
Medical history required	.39	.009	Not required—have not hired Required—have hired
Personal experience of employer with breast cancer	−.05	.392	——
Knowledge about breast cancer	.17	.165	——
Work experience of employer with breast cancer	.12	.246	——
Employer education	.47	.002	Less education—have not hired More education—have hired
Employer sex	−.35	.016	Male—hired; Female—not hired
Employer age	.04	.399	——

Responsibility for decision making (medical or non-medical) is dependent on company factors, primarily type of company and percentage of employees who are women, rather than policy factors such as sick leave. The type of decision maker (medical or non-medical) does not appear to be an important predictor of the hiring of a woman with a history of breast cancer.

TABLE 10.2
Predictors of Hiring Practice

Item	F	Beta	p	Implied Relationship
Company factors size company	8.64	.38	.025	≤ 225 employees—not hired > 225 employees—hired
Company policies sick leave (a)	12.89	− .51	.005	Low sick leave—hired High sick leave—not hired
Insurance (b)	4.49	.29	.05	Low insurance—not hired High insurance—hired
Employer Attributes education	9.46	.49	.025	Less education—not hired More education—hired
Sex	2.30	.24	NS	——
Age	2.40	.22	NS	——
Personal experience with women who have had breast cancer	4.27	− .28	.05	Less experience—hired More experience—not hired
Knowledge	.30	.08	NS	——
Total for the regression: r-q = .69; F = 6.36; degrees of freedom = 8/23; p < .001				

(a) Sick leave low = no paid sick leave days, no policy, some employees do not get sick leave, 10 or fewer days per year; high = 11 plus days per year
(b) Insurance low = company not involved or pays only part of premium for employees; high = company pays entire premium

Discussion

Though the factors entered into the regression model to explain hiring practices are those set forth in the theoretical model (Figure 10.1), some of the individual relationships to the dependent variable, as indicated by beta values, are surprising.

Knowledge about breast cancer does not seem to be a predictor of hiring decisions. Health educators and others have known for a long time that increasing knowledge or providing information to individuals about disease does not necessarily affect their own health behaviors or their behavior toward others. This lack of a relationship between knowledge and behavior seems to be borne out in this case as well. Both organizational factors, such as a company's size, and individual factors, such as employer's subjective experience with cancer patients, take precedence over the amount or accuracy of their knowledge about either the disease or the extent of its surgical disability when predicting hiring behavior. The smaller a company and the more personal experience an employer has with breast cancer, the less likely women with a history of this disease are to be hired.

Company policies regarding sick leave (number of paid sick leave days the company grants employees annually) and type of medical insurance (how involved the company is in payment of medical premiums) are also important predictors of hiring practices, *but they operate in opposite directions from one another*. That is, the more generous a company's sick leave benefits for its employees are, the *less* likely it is to hire a woman with breast cancer; however, the more comprehensive the medical insurance plan a company has for its employees, the *more* likely it is to hire such women.[2]

The fact that 69 percent of the variance in hiring is explained by company factors, policies, and the employer is noteworthy. The other factors in the model which could not be tested (women's individual medical and psychosocial conditions) almost certainly account for a substantial part of the remaining variance.

The model, we conclude, does have merit in explaining hiring practices for women with a history of breast cancer. Though some factors have been found to be stronger than others, the basic scheme of societal context, organizational level (company factors), and individual characteristics (of both employer and the applicant) appears to be a sound one.

Finally, the variable "decision-making responsibility (medical or non-medical)" essentially was erased from the model. It appears that regardless of the role of the final decision maker, the influence of factors other than the applicant's actual medical condition (e.g., a company's sick leave benefits or the employer's personal experience with cancer) is crucial when assessing an individual's suitability for employment.

The lack of specific model policies and the influence of the employer's personal experience suggest that subjective, rather than medical and company, criteria take precedence in the decision to hire individuals with past medical or surgical disabilities. Whether these same factors would predict a similar outcome in the case of women with other handicaps or medical conditions remains to be explored. Whether the same criteria would emerge as predictive of the hiring of men with similar medical histories (e.g., former cancer patients) is also problematic.

Conclusions

The results of this research indicate that the theoretical model developed to explain the decision to hire or not to hire women with a history of breast cancer can be a useful tool, especially in generating specific hypotheses to be tested by more rigorous future designs. That such a large amount of the variance in the dependent variable ("hiring practices") could be explained by organizational factors and the personal characteristics of the employer has at least two major implications.

First, the finding that the employer's personal experience with such women is an important element in whether they will be hired has disturbing discriminatory overtones. Subjective employment selection on the basis of personal experience is not only unfair to job applicants or employees but also to the company which loses potential workers. If medical criteria are used in hiring and/or firing, these standards should relate to individuals' abilities to perform specified jobs. That is, disability in the work place should be defined as a functional inability to perform in some areas (Davis, 1978). If occupational physicians or nurses *are* consulted or, likewise, personal physicians, they should be asked to make medical judgments about people's current physical conditions and whether they are capable of carrying out the jobs to be performed, rather than simply asked for a prognosis about the likelihood of future illnesses. The use of any other criteria suggest idiosyncratic standards which come dangerously close to the ofttimes ill-defined explanations used in rationalizing discriminatory practices based on racism, sexism, or ageism.

Hanks, in proposing nondiscriminatory medical standards, states: "If employees are medically capable of performing fully and safely work in question at time of hire, the only valid medical measure relative to current work-performance and risk has been met" (Hanks, 1977: 187). He goes further in suggesting that society must develop compensatory mechanisms that will relieve industry of part of the financial burden for degenerative and chronic disease for which it is presently held responsible. Insurance companies are also prime targets for remedial education and/or legislation. They set the rates which may influence employers to screen cancer patients differently on the basis of an expected (but not empirically confirmed) increase in absenteeism or a greater need for medical treatment.

Second, many of the determinants of the hiring decision are external to the individual woman with a history of breast cancer. Regardless of her particular condition, much of the decision about whether she is employed appears to be determined by factors beyond her control. Thus, rehabilitation programs which focus on preparing women with a history of breast cancer to return to work are inadequate at best, and inappropriate at worst. Education programs must aim at a target population larger than simply "cured" cancer patients.

Not only must they help prepare women who are able to work again after surgery to deal with potential deterrents in the employment situation arising from possible prejudices against them as cancer "carriers" or "handicapped" workers, but they must also work with employers in helping them apply nondiscriminatory medical standards. In addition, it is possible that returning *breast* cancer patients may face additional problems as a result not only of their medical condition but also, possibly, because they are women or, even more specifically, older women returning to the job market, often after an absence of many years.

As has been mentioned above, insurance companies are another target of educational programs if they are proceeding on outmoded medical knowledge, conservative survival rate statistics, or labor force statistics unadjusted for changes in women's roles. Davis has suggested that standards applied to the employment of the "medically handicapped" be based on an individual's record of disability days and crisis events, rather than on "disability category," a form of labeling which can affect whether medically handicapped persons are accepted into vocational, educational, or other programs (1978).

Since knowledge alone is not enough to effect the kinds of change proposed above, more research such as Alexander's (1975, 1977) must be done in order to demonstrate to employers that discriminatory medical standards are not in either the company's or the worker's best interests. The relationships between amount of sick leave taken, medical insurance costs to the company, and persons hired with certain disease conditions need to be studied further. Since the hiring decision appears to be influenced by employer attributes *rather than knowledge*, more in-depth work on reactions to the causes and consequences of a disease, rather than the amount or type of knowledge society has about it, needs to be undertaken.

Finally, the research reported here did not include a comparison group of male cancer patients. Future research which sought to address whether women with a history of breast cancer faced an additional source of discrimination merely because they were working women, and not only from the stigmatization or fear caused by the disease, should incorporate into the research design a similar group of male workers returning to old jobs or beginning new ones after a series of treatments or extensive surgery for cancer. There is no reason that similar research to that described here could not be used to tease apart the effects of gender, condition, and other factors (e.g., age) known to contribute to discriminatory hiring practices. While in the present study there appeared to be no effect of employer's sex on the variation observed in hiring practices, the number of women personnel managers in this sample was really too small to examine adequately the interaction between sex of employer and of cancer patient returning to work. A study incorporating this research question would also be an interesting extension of our work.

Notes

1. An earlier edition of this article was presented at the American Association of Public Opinion Research (AAPOR) in Roanoke, Virginia, June 1978. Special thanks go to two anonymous reviewers for their constructive critiques on the organization of the article in manuscript form.
2. A possible explanation for this seeming contradiction may be that since direct costs to the company for sick leave are much greater than the direct company cost for medical insurance, the financial risk of hiring someone with a history of breast cancer, when viewed in terms of effect on the company's insurance rates, may indeed be quite small. Further, if the insurance coverage is the minimum offered by the insurance underwriter, then the actual premium paid may be as small or smaller in those companies with fuller coverage but who pay only part of the premium (employees paying the other part). Thus, it may well be that those companies more likely to hire women with a history of breast cancer may actually pay the entire medical insurance premium for their employees, but it may be quite small; in turn, these may be the very companies which provide less generous sick leave benefits for their employees. The cost of premiums for group medical insurance, of course, is affected by many factors: the total number of employees; the percentage of employees who are women (acturial data are different for men and women); and the predominant type of employee (management and production employees, for example, are exposed to different kinds of health risks).

References

Alexander, R. W., A. S. Marda and R. J. Walker. 1975. "The validity of preemployment medical evaluations." *Journal of Occupational Medicine* 17: 687-92.

———, J. C. Brennan, A. S. Marda and R. J. Walker. 1977. "The value of preplacement medical examinations for nonhazardous light duty work." *Journal of Occupational Medicine* 19: 107-12.

California. 1975. Assembly Bill 1194, Chapter 431, Sections 1411-1412 of the Labor Code amended, approved by the Governor, August 28.

Craig, T. J., G. W. Comstock, and P. B. Geiser. 1974. "Quality of survival in breast cancer patients: A case controlled comparison." *Cancer* 33, No. 5: 1451-57.

Davis, C. 1978. Roundtable Report. *Women and Health Roundtable*: 2, No. 12.

Feldman, F. L. 1978. "Work and cancer health histories: A study of the experiences of recovered blue-collar workers." California Division, American Cancer Society, San Francisco, California.

Hanks, T. G. 1977. "Medical standards for employment in relation to non-discrimination laws." *Journal of Occupational Medicine* 19: 181-87.

Jenkins, C. D. and S. J. Zyzanski. 1968. "Dimensions of belief and feeling concerning three diseases—poliomyelitis, cancer, and mental illness: A factor analytic study." *Behavioral Science* 13: 372-81.

McKenna, R. J. 1974. "Employability and insurability of the cancer patient." A paper prepared for the American Cancer Society.

New York. 1973. Flynn Act, Chapter 988, Laws of 1974 in Regular Sessions, 1973-1974, March 6, 1973, 4524B.

Schottenfeld, D. and G. Robbins. 1970. "Quality of survival among patients who have had radical mastectomy." *Cancer* 26 (September): 651-55.

Tokarski, S. S., J. Skaezynski, L. Smith, and B. Seboda. 1976. "Not all illnesses are handicaps." *Employee Relations Law Journal* 2: 66-85.

Voelz, G. L. and J. H. Spiekard. 1975. "Preemployment medical evaluation by questionnaire." *Journal of Occupational Medicine* 17: 687-92.

Wakefield, J. 1970. "The social implications of cancer." *Radiography* 36: 93-5.

Weinstock, M. and J. Haft. 1974. "The effect of illness on employment opportunities." *Archives of Environmental Health* 29: 79-83.

Wheatley, G. H., W. R. Cunnick, B. P. Wright, and D. van Keuren. 1974. "The employment of persons with a history of treatment for cancer." *Cancer* 33: 441-45.

Williamson, S. M. 1971. "18 years experience without preemployment examinations." *Journal of Occupational Medicine* 13: 465-657.

11

Like Other Women: Perspectives of Mothers with Physical Disabilities

Susan Shaul, Pamela J. Dowling,
and Bernice F. Laden

*This article is based on interviews with 10 mothers, ranging in age from 19 to 45
and living in the Puget Sound area of Washington State. These women have neuro-
muscular or musculoskeletal disabilities, and their children range in age from 11
months to adulthood. The article focuses on specific issues and concerns regarding
early childhood management, and includes some discussion of prenatal and obstetrical
care. Common misconceptions concerning motherhood and disability are also discussed. Men with disabilities also have special concerns as parents. Although their
concerns are not addressed in this article, they are not seen as any less important or
less deserving of attention.*

Introduction

Until recently there has been a cultural bias that women with disabilities
cannot and should not bear and raise children. Consequently, family planning
services, obstetrical care, and early childhood guidance have often neglected
the needs of women with disabilities. Mainstreaming, implementation of
Section 503 and 504 of the national Rehabilitation Act of 1973, and other
new state and federal legislation have begun to have an impact on service
delivery to the disabled population, providing greater opportunities and increasingly complex choices. While many disabled women choose to pursue
careers, others want to direct their energies toward raising children, or combining career and family. However, society's attitude toward women with
disabilities has been slow to change.

This resistance has been reflected in the lack of literature available to parents
with disabilities. May (1974) discusses minor architectural adaptations and

recreational activities which mothers with physical disabilities might accomplish. Otherwise, American society, as reflected in the literature, has denied the existence of any special needs. This denial reflects the larger attitudinal barriers faced by people with disabilities.

The stigma of being disabled is difficult to erase. A disabled woman's capacity to be a partner in an intimate, sexual relationship and her physical ability to conceive and bear a child may be doubted by even her own family. Bogle and Shaul (1979) point out, "Many congenitally disabled women report that their parents programmed them to be 'super career' women in the belief that they would never be considered marriage material" (p. 39).

Societal resistance to viewing women with disabilities as potential parents comes from several different pervasive cultural myths:

Physically disabled women are extraordinarily dependent on other people. Many nondisabled people mistakenly assume that individuals with disabilities are unable to do basic maintenance for themselves, let alone a child. In reality, most physically disabled people lead independent, productive lives.

Physical disability is somehow contagious or inherited. This is a remnant of the belief that people with disabilities are sick or unhealthy. Only a small percentage of disabilities are genetically based.

Physically disabled people are asexual. Many nondisabled people often view sex as an acrobatic activity. This causes difficulty in understanding that physically disabled people are capable of enjoying warm, intimate relationships and being sexually active.

Being disabled is such a depressing and dreary existence that a disabled individual should not bring a child into that world. Few disabled people spend time dwelling on their disability. They are involved in working, homemaking, and the same activities that the general population enjoys.

Physical mobility is essential to child-rearing. Because disabled women have not been portrayed as mothers, it is difficult for the general population to understand how a child can be raised by a woman with mobility restrictions.

This study was therefore undertaken as a pilot project to investigate the needs of mothers with disabilities. Ten women in the Seattle area agreed to be interviewed. They were contacted through a previous research project (Shaul et al., 1978) and informal networking in the community. The women had chosen to become parents after they were disabled. Their disabilities included spinal cord injury, multiple sclerosis, post-polio and spina bifida. At the time of the interviews, their children ranged in age from 11 months to mid-30's. While clearly not representative of all women with disabilities who choose to become pregnant, these women were able to indicate potential areas of concern and needs from service providers.

Pre-Pregnancy

When deciding whether they want to become pregnant, most women with disabilities want to speak with a woman who has a similar disability. Many able-bodied women have relied on their mothers or friends to share what pregnancy and child-rearing are like, but disabled women often need more information and advice that is related to their specific disability.

> I really wanted to talk to another disabled woman who had gone through a pregnancy to find out what sort of things to anticipate during my pregnancy and after the baby was born. . . . I couldn't find anyone. . . . I think that networking among disabled women is just now beginning to grow. (paraplegic)

There are legitimate concerns as to how the physical stress of pregnancy may affect a disabled woman. For example, mobility, respiration, or elimination, perhaps not working at "normal" levels, will have the extra burden of the developing fetus.

At this point, many of these questions can be answered only by conjecture, as pregnant women with specific disabilities have not been studied. Health care professionals are not able to provide women with consistent answers. A woman with spina bifida told us:

> I talked to my doctor about becoming pregnant and he said absolutely not; so I talked to an obstetrician and he said I should have no problems. Confused, I talked to a third doctor and he told me I should get another opinion.

With expanded research, there will be increased professional awareness in the future, avoiding scenes that are still too common:

> The nurse looked at me, amazed. She said, laughing, "I guess I was just surprised you were really here for a pregnancy test." (quadriplegic)

Given the wide variety of attitudes found among health care providers, and inadequate information on pregnancy and disability, what are the experiences of mothers with disabilities really like?

Pregnancy, Labor, and Delivery

It is common for health providers to expect that pregnancy, being a somewhat disabling condition for many nondisabled women, will cause tremendous inconvenience for disabled women. Many of the women in our study had very few problems with mobility and self-care. One post-polio woman in our study, who is paraplegic and uses a wheelchair, worked until two weeks before her delivery; a woman with spina bifida stayed ambulatory (using crutches) until the delivery. Another woman (post-polio) who uses a wheelchair told us:

> As I got bigger and bigger, it became harder to get up on my knees to get my pants on . . . so I just started wearing long dresses and no underwear.

Experiences with labor and delivery were similar to those of nondisabled women. One of the 10 had a premature infant, two had deliveries by Caesarean section, and the others had relatively uncomplicated vaginal deliveries. The three complications mentioned related specifically to the pregnancy, and not to the women's disabilities.

The women interviewed found the support systems available to nondisabled expectant and newly delivered women valuable. For example, one woman with spina bifida benefited enormously from Lamaze classes. The woman who had a premature baby participated in a neonatal intensive care unit parents' support group.

Early Years

One of the most difficult periods for child management is the first few years of the child's life. During this time, physically caring for the baby or young child usually requires some environmental modifications. The mothers found few resources that were commercially available. One woman said that pre- and post-natally she had a physical therapist, social worker, and interested nursing student all looking for different mechanical aids to ease child care. They came back empty-handed.

Over time, each woman found various devices to ease transporting her child. For one woman with spina bifida it was an "Umbroller", a lightweight stroller that is easily collapsible and portable.

> The Umbroller was helpful because the baby doesn't have to be able to sit up. I'd walk a step, take my hand away from the crutch, push the stroller down the hall a few feet, walk a few more steps, and push it a little further.

Another woman's father came up with some physical modifications:

> My dad built a tray that snapped onto the arms of my wheelchair. The baby could be inside the tray and my arms would be free to push my chair. I also used a portable bassinet with wheels that allowed me to push the baby from room to room. For a changing table, we took the short legs off an old coffee table and replaced them with long legs that raised the baby to just the right height. (paraplegic)

Going out alone is somewhat difficult for many new mothers, but it is aggravated by the encumbrance of disability. For a woman who uses a wheelchair, an infant can mark a temporary end to being able to travel around independently. It is difficult to push a wheelchair around shopping centers while holding onto an active child in your lap.

Getting a baby in and out of a car can be another major obstacle to going out.

> The biggest restriction I found during that time was the difficulty in taking him somewhere by myself. I have been driving since I was 16 and it was the first time my driving . . . independence had been restricted. I enter the car on the passenger side and slide over to the driver's seat. It was difficult to manage baby, car seat, and wheel chair. So until he learned to walk, I usually had a family member or friend accompany us on our outings. (paraplegic)

It is likely, too, that daily child management requires more energy from disabled women, which can lead to exhaustion. This period seemed to end for the women when relieved of a share of the responsibility. For one family in our study, the pediatrician recommended a "24-hour break for Mom, once a week," when the child would go to his grandparents. In other families, it was pre-school that enabled the mother to think about her own goals again, contact friends, and rebuild intimacy with her husband. All of the husbands had provided significant help with household chores, as well as child management. Several worked evenings, giving a handy break to the mothers during the day by helping out with dinner, dishes, calming temper tantrums, and organizing playtime activities.

Discipline

In the area of discipline, the families had adapted to the "givens" in the situation and had found ingenious solutions. Primary for everyone was the understanding that verbal commands are law. This was not always easy to do, but families had various ways of enforcing verbal authority.

> I depend a lot on voice control. She has to come to my commands. I can't pick her up every time she falls because maybe the chair isn't positioned right. Once she fell off her trike on the ramp and there was no way I could come out and get her untangled. She realized that and got herself untangled. She's just more aware of voice control. She has to be able to understand. (woman with multiple sclerosis)

One woman said that the best advice she had received was from her pediatrician, who reommended that she only make demands that she could enforce and be much more selective about what she was demanding of the child.

Developing authority behind verbal commands is often difficult for the parent with a disability because of the intermittent reinforcement of limit-testing with the nondisabled parent or other nondisabled people. For instance, one mother had very few discipline problems until her daughter went to a preschool where the teachers were very physical in restraining the children and often did things for the little girl she was capable of doing herself. Similarly, relatives or other interested people would pick her up when she was misbehaving. Then she came home and started testing already determined limits.

> I'd say to my friends, "I have to rely on voice commands and when you walk over and do something for her or pick her up, you're really putting a crunch on me, because then she expects me to do it." (quadriplegic)

The choice is made very early whether to keep the child confined within reach (which none of the parents had chosen) or give the child reasonable freedom while trusting in their survival skills. The children's adaptive capabilities are dramatic: they learn to climb on Mom's lap when hurt, reach up to be lifted out of a crib, or hold onto a wheelchair when crossing the street as it if were Mom's hand.

> I emphasized early how important it was to listen to what I said because there would be times I might not be able to get to him to help him out of a jam. He seemed to understand that. He is very good at listening to me about not going into the street, straying away in stores, or going someplace I may not be able to get to. But when it comes time for dinner, bedtime, or bath, he is like any other child and heads in the opposite direction! (paraplegic)

Some problems were eased by environmental revisions. Homes with disabled adults often have fewer pieces of furniture, as they restrict mobility. This cuts down on the number of obstacles for a toddler. Traditional environment revisions included safety plugs in sockets, glassware put away, deadbolt locks (so the child could not get in and out to the street independently), fenced-in yards, and other toddler proofing mechanisms.

As mentioned earlier, child-rearing is far from a fait accompli for the able-bodied population. All mothers have questions regarding appropriate discipline techniques.

> You have to remind yourself that your disability really has nothing to do with whatever the problem is at hand . . . you know, it's a parent-child thing, not a disabled parent-child thing. (woman with multiple sclerosis)

Unfortunately, women with disabilities are placed in a double-bind. On the one hand they are told "you couldn't possibly raise children and discipline them well," and on the other, when everything turns out all right, they hear, "Well, dear, your child *had* to be good."

> Boy, does that make me mad! It's baloney! Kids aren't good because they have to be. They're good because of the effort and love you put into them . . . if you're lucky. (quadriplegic)

Advantages and Disadvantages

At one point during the interview, we asked each woman, "Can you think of any advantages to being a disabled parent?" Most stressed that their children had an increased sense of independence because the child knew that some things wouldn't be done for him/her. Mothers mentioned that their children were getting dressed by themselves earlier, learning about keys and locks, getting food for themselves, and genuinely being helpful before their peers in nondisabled households. Most were concerned that this not be too oppressive:

> I don't like kids to have to help their parents because of their disability. I don't want him waiting on me. I don't need that. I don't want him to think he has to do that for me. (woman with spina bifida)

Disability was often the stimulus to encourage independence in children for philosophical, as well as practical, reasons:

> We were always very strict with the kids. We thought, "What if something happened to my husband or maybe we'd both die!" The polio brought it closer to you that you might die, so we tried to get the kids to be very responsible for themselves, and I think they were quite adult for their ages. (paraplegic)

Another advantage that the women cited was their children's increased sensitivity to other stigmatized individuals. Sometimes this took the form of defending or befriending "picked-on" children who were classmates, or not caring if someone "looked a little different." Most of the mothers had had the experience of being "defended" by their child to the world at large:

> One time we were in a cafeteria-type place and this woman kept staring and staring at me. Finally, my daughter (aged 20) needed to walk by this stranger and my daughter said, "You know, it's not nice to stare!" When she told me, I said, "You didn't!", and she said, "I sure did!" and we laughed and laughed. (quadriplegic)

The women were also able to cite some disadvantages to being disabled and a parent. The most significant disadvantage seemed to be that various family activities were difficult or impossible to participate in. One mother talked about not being able to attend a school play one of her children was in because the school was not accessible and she couldn't find any help that day. For a quadriplegic woman, there was the sadness of not being able to teach her daughter how to use scissors or a hammer. One of the paraplegic women said, "How can I teach him how to play hopscotch or swim?" Most of the mothers acknowledged other people are available to help with these activities (father, grandparents, friends, aunts or uncles), but that they nonetheless feel a sense of loss.

Extended absences from their children because of medical needs were also disadvantages. This varies with the nature of the disability, being more of a concern with progressive disabilities.

> My daughter is constantly afraid I'm going to leave her and go back to the hospital for some complication or another of the multiple sclerosis. (woman with multiple sclerosis)

For those women injured after their children are already born, there is often a long readjustment period when they re-enter the home—a readjustment to Mom being back and then another to her being "different".

As children of mothers with disabilities come into contact with their peers, there may be an initial tension with the other children from having a mother who is different. One woman related an incident where her first-grader came home in tears. When he was able to tell her what had happened, he told her that he didn't want her to come to school anymore because all the kids made fun of the way she walked and he was the only kid with a Mom who was "different". After comforting him, she spoke to his teacher and made arrangements to come to school and do a little "inservice" with the kids, allowing them to ask questions and get to know her as Joey's Mom, instead of only as the "woman who walks funny."

Recommendations

Through this survey of women, many unmet needs became obvious. The following recommendations are based on concerns expressed by women with disabilities.

Pre-pregnancy counseling. Compiling experiences of mothers who are disabled and making the information available would be beneficial to women with disabilities contemplating motherhood. Peer groups or individual peer counselors could be made available for disabled women.

Human service professionals need additional training in the area of disability and pregnancy so they will be better equipped to answer questions posed by disabled women. Institutions of higher education and health care education programs could incorporate a module on sexuality, pregnancy and disability. Perhaps having a disabled mother visit classes to share experiences would be helpful to potential health care providers.

Prenatal/obstetrical care. More training and information on pregnancy and disability needs to be available in medical school curriculum so there will be more physicians available to give obstetrical care to women with disabilities in a comfortable and knowledgeable manner. Lamaze and other childbirth preparation classes should be held in accessible meeting places and be made available to disabled women.

Child management. Resource listings of adaptive devices or suggestions which would make child management easier should be developed and updated in a central clearinghouse. A support group of disabled mothers would foster sharing resources.

Research. Too much in the areas of female sexuality, reproduction, and parenting, at this point, is conjecture. Further research on medical implications of pregnancy and social implications of disabled parents is needed.

The technology of rehabilitation needs to catch up with the technology of obstetrics. There must be ways to make child care easier for disabled parents. As one woman said, "They invented the wheelchair. Surely they can invent an attachment to transport a child." Such "convenience" devices would have a tremendous positive impact for parents with disabilities.

Summary

The traditional role of women as mothers is one of sole caretaker and nurturer of her children (i.e., feeding, dressing, chauffeuring, nursing, and disciplining). Although this image is in the process of change, it is still one which society uses as its reference point. Since disabled persons are often seen as "sick," and in need of being taken care of, it is difficult for society to understand how a mother with a disability can fit the active nurturer/caretaker role. The majority of people have a hard time imagining how people with disabilities function and take care of themselves, let alone their children. As more and more disabled people enter the mainstream of life through employment, recreation, education and media representation, the myths surrounding disability will begin to lessen.

The strengths and capabilities of the women we spoke with were striking. They, like able-bodied parents, felt that children dramatically change one's life and that frustrations can result. They more often experienced limitations as to how much they could participate in their children's activities. But, like most parents, they said they were glad children were part of their lives.

As society's expectations for mothers change, women in general are finding more parenting and support system options available to them (i.e., shared responsibility for child-rearing with partner or extended family, daycare centers, single parenting). Not only does the disabled mother benefit from these options, but she has a wealth of information and expertise to add to the spectrum of parenting. Although there are unique concerns that merit special attention for mothers with disabilities, once these concerns are successfully addressed, more women with disabilities will be able to enjoy the option of motherhood. As one woman reflected:

> You don't need a body that is physically "perfect" to be a good mother . . . environments need to be modified and support systems worked out, but the most important qualification for parenting has nothing to do with physical perfection. It has to do with love, warmth, and a willingness to share that with a child. It has to do with being human and that is something we all share.

Note

Work on this article was made possible under Grant #10H530081032 from the Department of Health and Human Services, Bureau of Community Health Services, Family Planning Program, 1980.

References

Bogle, J. and S. Shaul. 1979. "Still a Woman, Still a Man." *Journal of Current Social Issues* (Spring): 39-41.

Goffman, E. 1963. *Stigma: Notes on the Management of Spoiled Identity*. Englewood Cliffs, N. J.: Prentice Hall.

May, E. E., Neva R. Waggoner, and Eleanor Boettke. 1974. *Independent Living for the Handicapped and the Elderly*. Boston: Houghton Mifflin Company.

Shaul, S., J. Bogle, A. Norman, and J. Hale-Harbaugh. 1978. *Toward Intimacy: Family Planning and Sexuality Concerns of Physically Disabled Women*. New York: Human Sciences Press.

Contributors

Adrienne Asch is senior human rights specialist at the New York State Division of Human Rights, staff therapist of the Institute for Contemporary Psychotherapy and adjunct assistant professor at Barnard College. She has published articles on industrial social work, women with disabilities, therapists with disabilities, and the disability rights movement.

Gaylene Becker is assistant director of the Aging Health Policy Center and assistant adjunct professor of medical anthropology and social and behavioral sciences, the University of California—San Francisco. She is the author of *Growing Old in Silence* (1983) and coeditor, with Lerita Coleman and Stephen Ainlay, of *Stigma: An Interdisciplinary Approach* (1984).

Emily Bonwich is program evaluation coordinator at the Howard A. Rusk Rehabilitation Center, the University of Missouri—Columbia Health Sciences Center; and adjunct assistant professor in the Department of Physical Medicine and Rehabilitation. She has published and presented her work nationally on social and psychological factors related to rehospitalization after spinal cord injury, education for spinal cord injury prevention, and community health issues.

Nancy A. Brooks is assistant professor of sociology at Wichita State University. She is the coauthor, with Jeffrey Riemer, of *Framing the Artist: A Social Portrait of Midwestern Artists* (1982). She has also published numerous articles on chronic illness and physical disability and conducted observations of disability programs in European and Scandinavian countries.

Mary Jo Deegan is associate professor of sociology at the University of Nebraska—Lincoln. She has published numerous articles on physical rehabilitation, the history of women in sociology, contemporary theory, and popular culture. She is the author of *Jane Adams and the Men of the Chicago School* (Transaction, forthcoming).

Pamela J. Dowling is coordinator of the Employment Connection at the University of Washington and the owner of Northwest Consultants in Seattle, Washington. She has an extensive background in the employment and training needs of disabled persons and is a consultant in the area of sexuality and disability.

Jo Anne L. Earp is medical sociologist in the Department of Health Education at the University of North Carolina. In 1983 she received the McGavran Award for excellence in teaching from the University of North Carolina. Her research focuses on women's health and patient education issues as well as research methodologies.

Michelle Fine is assistant professor of psychology and education at the University of Pennsylvannia. She is a rape counselor and reproductive rights activist.

Heather L. Gray is interim coordinator of the Southern Regional Jobs for Peace Campaign. Until recently she was a research specialist at the Emory University Center for Rehabilitation Medicine. She has several publications on end-stage renal disease and on aging male homosexuals.

Joanne K. Jauregui is an educator and social service provider who is an active participant in many aspects of deaf community life. She has developed and produced television programs for the deaf community in the Bay Area of California since 1981. Until that time she was an active member of the Center for Independent Living, Berkeley, where she was an integral part of facilitating independence for deaf and hearing-impaired persons.

Cynthia Kolb is director of Disabled Students' Services at San Franciso State University. She has published in the areas of adjustment to disability and adult therapy. She was previously the president of the National Association on Handicapped Students in Post-Secondary Education.

Nancy G. Kutner is assistant professor of rehabilitation medicine at the Emory University School of Medicine. She has been the principal investigator for three federally funded grants focusing on the disabled and published numerous articles on disability. In 1983 she was honored with the Research Award of the National Kidney Foundation of Georgia.

Elizabeth Kutza is associate professor at the School of Social Service Administration at the University of Chicago. In 1983-84 she received a Robert Wood Johnson Health Policy Fellowship. She is the author of *The Benefits of Old Age* (1981), and has numerous publications on long-term care and income maintenance for the elderly. She was a presenter at the White House Conference on Aging in 1981.

Bernice F. Laden is a consultant for Northwest Consultants in Seattle, Washington, and a free-lance consultant and instructor at A.S.U.W. Experimental College.

Nancy McCharen is presently at the Yaounde, Cameroons, Public Health Service, serving as an educator advisor. She has publications in health education and extensive service as a Peace Corps volunteer and staff member.

Marsha Saxton is director of Consultation and Training at the Boston Self Help Center. She has done pioneering work and writings in the fields of peer counseling and women and disability. She was a contributing editor to *Our Bodies, Ourselves* (rev. 1983).

Susan Shaul, a psychologist, is the author of *Within Reach: Providing Family Planning Services to Physically Disabled Women* (1978), and coauthor, with Julia Hale-Harbugh, Ann Duecy Norman, and Jane Bogle of *Toward Intimacy: Family Planning and Sexuality Concerns of Physically Disabled Women* (1978).